www.EffortlessMath.com

... So Much More Online!

✓ FREE Math lessons

✓ More Math learning books!

✓ Mathematics Worksheets

✓ Online Math Tutors

Need a PDF version of this book?

Please visit www.EffortlessMath.com

GED Math
Study Guide
2020 - 2021

A Comprehensive Review and Step-By-Step Guide to Preparing for the GED Math

By

Reza Nazari & Ava Ross

All inquiries should be addressed to:

info@effortlessMath.com

www.EffortlessMath.com

ISBN: 978-1-64612-220-2

Published by: Effortless Math Education

www.EffortlessMath.com

Visit www.EffortlessMath.com

for Online Math Practice

Description

GED Math Study Guide, which reflects the 2020 - 2021 test guidelines, is designed by top GED Math instructors and test prep experts to help test takers succeed on the GED Math Test. The updated version of this comprehensive GED Math preparation book includes Math lessons, extensive exercises, sample GED Math questions, and quizzes with answers and detailed solutions to help you hone your math skills, overcome your exam anxiety, boost your confidence—and do your best to ace the GED exam on test day. Upon completion of this perfect GED Math prep book, you will have a solid foundation and sufficient practice to ace the GED Math test.

Not only does this all-inclusive prep book offer everything you will ever need to prepare for the GED Math test, but it also contains two complete and realistic GED Math tests that reflect the format and question types on the GED to help you check your exam-readiness and identify where you need more practice.

GED Math Study Guide contains many exciting and unique features to help you prepare for the GED Math test, including:

- ✓ Content 100% aligned with the 2020 GED® test
- ✓ Written by GED Math instructors and test experts
- ✓ Complete coverage of all GED Math concepts and topics which you will be tested
- ✓ Step-by-step guide for all GED Math topics
- ✓ Abundant Math skill building exercises to help test-takers approach different question types that might be unfamiliar to them
- ✓ Exercises on different GED Math topics such as integers, percent, equations, polynomials, exponents and radicals
- ✓ 2 full-length practice tests (featuring new question types) with detailed answers

This GED Math prep book and other Effortless Math Education books are used by thousands of students each year to help them review core content areas, brush-up in math, discover their strengths and weaknesses, and achieve their best scores on the GED test.

Contents

Name:	Date: ....

Topic	Simplifying Fractions
Notes	✓ Evenly divide both the top and bottom of the fraction by $2, 3, 5, 7, \ldots$ etc. ✓ Continue until you can't go any further.
Example	*Simplify* $\frac{36}{48}$ To simplify $\frac{36}{48}$, find a number that both 36 and 48 are divisible by. Both are divisible by 12. Then: $\frac{36}{48} = \frac{36 \div 12}{48 \div 12} = \frac{3}{4}$
Your Turn!	1) $\frac{2}{18} =$ 2) $\frac{22}{66} =$ 3) $\frac{12}{48} =$ 4) $\frac{11}{99} =$ 5) $\frac{15}{75} =$ 6) $\frac{25}{100} =$ 7) $\frac{16}{72} =$ 8) $\frac{32}{96} =$ 9) $\frac{14}{77} =$ 10) $\frac{60}{84} =$

Name:	Date: ....

Topic	**Simplifying Fractions - Answers**
Notes	✓ Evenly divide both the top and bottom of the fraction by $2, 3, 5, 7, \ldots$ etc. ✓ Continue until you can't go any further.
Example	**Simplify** $\frac{36}{48}$ To simplify $\frac{36}{48}$, find a number that both 36 and 48 are divisible by. Both are divisible by 12. Then: $\frac{36}{48} = \frac{36 \div 12}{48 \div 12} = \frac{3}{4}$

Your Turn!	1) $\frac{2}{18} = \frac{1}{9}$	2) $\frac{22}{66} = \frac{1}{3}$
	3) $\frac{12}{48} = \frac{1}{4}$	4) $\frac{11}{99} = \frac{1}{9}$
	5) $\frac{15}{75} = \frac{1}{5}$	6) $\frac{25}{100} = \frac{1}{4}$
	7) $\frac{16}{72} = \frac{2}{9}$	8) $\frac{32}{96} = \frac{1}{3}$
	9) $\frac{14}{77} = \frac{2}{11}$	10) $\frac{60}{84} = \frac{5}{7}$

Name:	Date: ....

Topic	**Adding and Subtracting Fractions**
Notes	✓ For "like" fractions (fractions with the same denominator), add or subtract the numerators and write the answer over the common denominator. ✓ Find equivalent fractions with the same denominator before you can add or subtract fractions with different denominators. ✓ Adding and Subtracting with the same denominator: $$\frac{a}{b}+\frac{c}{b}=\frac{a+c}{b} \ , \ \frac{a}{b}-\frac{c}{b}=\frac{a-c}{b}$$ ✓ Adding and Subtracting fractions with different denominators: $$\frac{a}{b}+\frac{c}{d}=\frac{ad+bc}{bd} , \frac{a}{b}-\frac{c}{d}=\frac{ad-bc}{bd}$$
Example	*Find the sum.* $\frac{3}{5}+\frac{2}{3}=\frac{(3)3+(5)(2)}{5\times3}=\frac{19}{15}$ *Subtract.* $\frac{4}{7}-\frac{3}{7}=\frac{1}{7}$
Your Turn!	1) $\frac{3}{5}+\frac{2}{7}=$ 2) $\frac{7}{9}-\frac{4}{7}=$ 3) $\frac{4}{9}+\frac{5}{8}=$ 4) $\frac{5}{8}-\frac{2}{5}=$ 5) $\frac{2}{5}+\frac{1}{6}=$ 6) $\frac{2}{3}-\frac{1}{4}=$ 7) $\frac{8}{9}+\frac{5}{7}=$ 8) $\frac{6}{7}-\frac{5}{9}=$

Name:	Date: ....

Topic	**Adding and Subtracting Fractions - Answers**	
Notes	✓ For "like" fractions (fractions with the same denominator), add or subtract the numerators and write the answer over the common denominator. ✓ Find equivalent fractions with the same denominator before you can add or subtract fractions with different denominators. ✓ Adding and Subtracting with the same denominator: $$\frac{a}{b} + \frac{c}{b} = \frac{a+c}{b}, \quad \frac{a}{b} - \frac{c}{b} = \frac{a-c}{b}$$ ✓ Adding and Subtracting fractions with different denominators: $$\frac{a}{b} + \frac{c}{d} = \frac{ad+bc}{bd}, \frac{a}{b} - \frac{c}{d} = \frac{ad-bc}{bd}$$	
Example	***Find the sum.*** $\frac{3}{5} + \frac{2}{3} = \frac{(3)3+(5)(2)}{5\times 3} = \frac{19}{15}$ ***Subtract.*** $\frac{4}{7} - \frac{3}{7} = \frac{1}{7}$	
Your Turn!	1) $\frac{3}{5} + \frac{2}{7} = \frac{31}{35}$	2) $\frac{7}{9} - \frac{4}{7} = \frac{13}{63}$
	3) $\frac{4}{9} + \frac{5}{8} = \frac{77}{72}$	4) $\frac{5}{8} - \frac{2}{5} = \frac{9}{40}$
	5) $\frac{2}{5} + \frac{1}{6} = \frac{17}{30}$	6) $\frac{2}{3} - \frac{1}{4} = \frac{5}{12}$
	7) $\frac{8}{9} + \frac{5}{7} = \frac{101}{63}$	8) $\frac{6}{7} - \frac{5}{9} = \frac{19}{63}$

| **Name:** .... | **Date:** .... |

Topic	**Multiplying and Dividing Fractions**
Notes	✓ Multiplying fractions: multiply the top numbers and multiply the bottom numbers. ✓ Dividing fractions: Keep, Change, Flip Keep first fraction, change division sign to multiplication, and flip the numerator and denominator of the second fraction. Then, solve!
Examples	*Multiply.* $\frac{2}{5} \times \frac{3}{4} =$ Multiply the top numbers and multiply the bottom numbers. $\frac{2}{5} \times \frac{3}{4} = \frac{2\times3}{5\times4} = \frac{6}{20}$, simplify: $\frac{6}{2} = \frac{6\div2}{20\div2} = \frac{3}{10}$ *Divide.* $\frac{2}{5} \div \frac{3}{4} =$ Keep first fraction, change division sign to multiplication, and flip the numerator and denominator of the second fraction. Then: $\frac{2}{5} \div \frac{3}{4} = \frac{2}{5} \times \frac{4}{3} = \frac{2\times4}{5\times3} = \frac{8}{15}$
Your Turn!	1) $\frac{5}{9} \times \frac{4}{7} =$ 2) $\frac{3}{5} \div \frac{2}{3} =$ 3) $\frac{2}{7} \times \frac{3}{5} =$ 4) $\frac{2}{5} \div \frac{7}{12} =$ 5) $\frac{1}{7} \times \frac{4}{9} =$ 6) $\frac{2}{9} \div \frac{3}{7} =$ 7) $\frac{2}{5} \times \frac{6}{7} =$ 8) $\frac{1}{4} \div \frac{2}{5} =$

Name:	Date: ....

Topic	**Multiplying and Dividing Fractions - Answers**
Notes	✓ Multiplying fractions: multiply the top numbers and multiply the bottom numbers. ✓ Dividing fractions: Keep, Change, Flip Keep first fraction, change division sign to multiplication, and flip the numerator and denominator of the second fraction. Then, solve!
Examples	*Multiply.* $\frac{2}{5} \times \frac{3}{4} =$ Multiply the top numbers and multiply the bottom numbers. $\frac{2}{5} \times \frac{3}{4} = \frac{2\times3}{5\times4} = \frac{6}{20}$, simplify: $\frac{6}{2} = \frac{6\div2}{20\div2} = \frac{3}{10}$ *Divide.* $\frac{2}{5} \div \frac{3}{4} =$ Keep first fraction, change division sign to multiplication, and flip the numerator and denominator of the second fraction. Then: $\frac{2}{5} \div \frac{3}{4} = \frac{2}{5} \times \frac{4}{3} = \frac{2\times4}{5\times3} = \frac{8}{15}$
Your Turn!	1) $\frac{5}{9} \times \frac{4}{7} = \frac{20}{63}$ 2) $\frac{3}{5} \div \frac{2}{3} = \frac{9}{10}$ 3) $\frac{2}{7} \times \frac{3}{5} = \frac{6}{35}$ 4) $\frac{2}{5} \div \frac{7}{12} = \frac{24}{35}$ 5) $\frac{1}{7} \times \frac{4}{9} = \frac{4}{63}$ 6) $\frac{2}{9} \div \frac{3}{7} = \frac{14}{27}$ 7) $\frac{2}{5} \times \frac{6}{7} = \frac{12}{35}$ 8) $\frac{1}{4} \div \frac{2}{5} = \frac{5}{8}$

Name: ....

Date: ....

Topic	Adding Mixed Numbers
Notes	Use the following steps for adding mixed numbers. ✓ Add whole numbers of the mixed numbers. ✓ Add the fractions of each mixed number. ✓ Find the Least Common Denominator (LCD) if necessary. ✓ Add whole numbers and fractions. ✓ Write your answer in lowest terms.
Example	***Add mixed numbers.*** $1\frac{1}{2} + 2\frac{2}{3} =$ Rewriting our equation with parts separated, $1 + \frac{1}{2} + 2 + \frac{2}{3}$ Add whole numbers: $1 + 2 = 3$ Add fractions: $\frac{1}{2} + \frac{2}{3} = \frac{3}{6} + \frac{4}{6} = \frac{7}{6} = 1\frac{1}{6}$, Now, combine the whole and fraction parts: $3 + 1 + \frac{1}{6} = 4\frac{1}{6}$
Your Turn!	1) $1\frac{1}{12} + 2\frac{3}{4} =$ 2) $3\frac{5}{8} + 1\frac{1}{4} =$ 3) $1\frac{1}{10} + 2\frac{2}{5} =$ 4) $2\frac{5}{6} + 2\frac{2}{9} =$ 5) $2\frac{2}{7} + 1\frac{2}{21} =$ 6) $1\frac{3}{8} + 3\frac{2}{3} =$ 7) $3\frac{1}{5} + 1\frac{2}{8} =$ 8) $3\frac{1}{2} + 2\frac{3}{7} =$

Name:	Date: ....

Topic	**Adding Mixed Numbers - Answers**	
Notes	Use the following steps for adding mixed numbers. ✓ Add whole numbers of the mixed numbers. ✓ Add the fractions of each mixed number. ✓ Find the Least Common Denominator (LCD) if necessary. ✓ Add whole numbers and fractions. ✓ Write your answer in lowest terms.	
Example	***Add mixed numbers.*** $1\frac{1}{2} + 2\frac{2}{3} =$ Rewriting our equation with parts separated, $1 + \frac{1}{2} + 2 + \frac{2}{3}$ Add whole numbers: $1 + 2 = 3$ Add fractions: $\frac{1}{2} + \frac{2}{3} = \frac{3}{6} + \frac{4}{6} = \frac{7}{6} = 1\frac{1}{6}$ Now, combine the whole and fraction parts: $3 + 1 + \frac{1}{6} = 4\frac{1}{6}$	
Your Turn!	1) $1\frac{1}{12} + 2\frac{3}{4} = 3\frac{5}{6}$	2) $3\frac{5}{8} + 1\frac{1}{4} = 4\frac{7}{8}$
	3) $1\frac{1}{10} + 2\frac{2}{5} = 3\frac{1}{2}$	4) $2\frac{5}{6} + 2\frac{2}{9} = 5\frac{1}{18}$
	5) $2\frac{2}{7} + 1\frac{2}{21} = 3\frac{8}{21}$	6) $1\frac{3}{8} + 3\frac{2}{3} = 5\frac{1}{24}$
	7) $3\frac{1}{5} + 1\frac{2}{8} = 4\frac{9}{20}$	8) $3\frac{1}{2} + 2\frac{3}{7} = 5\frac{13}{14}$

Name: ....   Date: ....

Topic	Subtracting Mixed Numbers
Notes	Use the following steps for subtracting mixed numbers. ✓ Convert mixed numbers into improper fractions. $a\dfrac{c}{b} = \dfrac{ab+c}{b}$ ✓ Find equivalent fractions with the same denominator for unlike fractions (fractions with different denominators) ✓ Subtract the second fraction from the first one. ✓ Write your answer in lowest terms and convert it into a mixed number if the answer is an improper fraction.
Example	***Subtract.*** $5\dfrac{1}{2} - 2\dfrac{2}{3} =$ Convert mixed numbers into fractions: $5\dfrac{1}{2} = \dfrac{5\times2+1}{5} = \dfrac{11}{2}$ and $2\dfrac{2}{3} = \dfrac{2\times3+2}{4} = \dfrac{8}{3}$, these two fractions are "unlike" fractions. (they have different denominators). Find equivalent fractions with the same denominator. Use this formula: $\dfrac{a}{b} - \dfrac{c}{d} = \dfrac{ad-bc}{bd}$ $\dfrac{11}{2} - \dfrac{8}{3} = \dfrac{(11)(3)-(2)(8)}{2\times3} = \dfrac{33-16}{6} = \dfrac{17}{6}$, the answer is an improper fraction, convert it into a mixed number. $\dfrac{17}{6} = 2\dfrac{5}{6}$
Your Turn!	1) $2\dfrac{2}{5} - 1\dfrac{1}{3} =$ 2) $3\dfrac{5}{8} - 2\dfrac{1}{3} =$ 3) $6\dfrac{1}{4} - 1\dfrac{2}{7} =$ 4) $8\dfrac{2}{3} - 1\dfrac{1}{4} =$ 5) $8\dfrac{3}{4} - 1\dfrac{3}{8} =$ 6) $2\dfrac{3}{8} - 1\dfrac{2}{3} =$ 7) $13\dfrac{2}{7} - 1\dfrac{2}{21} =$ 8) $5\dfrac{1}{2} - 2\dfrac{3}{7} =$

Name:	Date: ....

Topic	**Subtracting Mixed Numbers - Answers**	
Notes	Use the following steps for subtracting mixed numbers. ✓ Convert mixed numbers into improper fractions. $a\frac{c}{b} = \frac{ab+c}{b}$ ✓ Find equivalent fractions with the same denominator for unlike fractions (fractions with different denominators) ✓ Subtract the second fraction from the first one. ✓ Write your answer in lowest terms and convert it into a mixed number if the answer is an improper fraction.	
Example	***Subtract.*** $5\frac{1}{2} - 2\frac{2}{3} =$ Convert mixed numbers into fractions: $5\frac{1}{2} = \frac{5\times 2+1}{5} = \frac{11}{2}$ and $2\frac{2}{3} = \frac{2\times 3+2}{4} = \frac{8}{3}$, these two fractions are "unlike" fractions. (they have different denominators). Find equivalent fractions with the same denominator. Use this formula: $\frac{a}{b} - \frac{c}{d} = \frac{ad-bc}{bd}$ $\frac{11}{2} - \frac{8}{3} = \frac{(11)(3)-(2)(8)}{2\times 3} = \frac{33-16}{6} = \frac{17}{6}$, the answer is an improper fraction, convert it into a mixed number. $\frac{17}{6} = 2\frac{5}{6}$	
Your Turn!	1) $2\frac{2}{5} - 1\frac{1}{3} = 1\frac{1}{15}$	2) $3\frac{5}{8} - 2\frac{1}{3} = 1\frac{7}{24}$
	3) $6\frac{1}{4} - 1\frac{2}{7} = 4\frac{27}{28}$	4) $8\frac{2}{3} - 1\frac{1}{4} = 7\frac{5}{12}$
	5) $8\frac{3}{4} - 1\frac{3}{8} = 7\frac{3}{8}$	6) $2\frac{3}{8} - 1\frac{2}{3} = \frac{17}{24}$
	7) $13\frac{2}{7} - 1\frac{2}{21} = 12\frac{4}{21}$	8) $5\frac{1}{2} - 2\frac{3}{7} = 3\frac{1}{14}$

Name: ....   Date: ....

Topic	Multiplying Mixed Numbers
Notes	✓ Convert the mixed numbers into fractions. $a\frac{c}{b} = a + \frac{c}{b} = \frac{ab+c}{b}$ ✓ Multiply fractions and simplify if necessary. $\frac{a}{b} \times \frac{c}{d} = \frac{a \times c}{b \times d}$ ✓ If the answer is an improper fraction (numerator is bigger than denominator), convert it into a mixed number.
Example	**Multiply** $2\frac{1}{4} \times 3\frac{1}{2}$ Convert mixed numbers into fractions: $2\frac{1}{4} = \frac{2 \times 4 + 1}{4} = \frac{9}{4}$ and $3\frac{1}{2} = \frac{3 \times 2 + 1}{2} = \frac{7}{2}$ Multiply two fractions: $\frac{9}{4} \times \frac{7}{2} = \frac{9 \times 7}{4 \times 2} = \frac{63}{8}$ The answer is an improper fraction. Convert it into a mixed number: $$\frac{63}{8} = 7\frac{7}{8}$$

Your Turn!	1) $5\frac{2}{3} \times 2\frac{2}{9} =$	2) $4\frac{1}{6} \times 5\frac{3}{7} =$
	3) $3\frac{1}{3} \times 3\frac{3}{4} =$	4) $2\frac{2}{9} \times 6\frac{1}{3} =$
	5) $2\frac{2}{7} \times 4\frac{3}{5} =$	6) $1\frac{4}{7} \times 9\frac{1}{2} =$
	7) $4\frac{1}{8} \times 3\frac{2}{3} =$	8) $6\frac{2}{3} \times 1\frac{1}{4} =$

Name:	Date: ....

Topic	**Multiplying Mixed Numbers - Answers**
Notes	✓ Convert the mixed numbers into fractions. $a\dfrac{c}{b} = a + \dfrac{c}{b} = \dfrac{ab+c}{b}$ ✓ Multiply fractions and simplify if necessary. $\dfrac{a}{b} \times \dfrac{c}{d} = \dfrac{a \times c}{b \times d}$ ✓ If the answer is an improper fraction (numerator is bigger than denominator), convert it into a mixed number.
Example	***Multiply*** $2\dfrac{1}{4} \times 3\dfrac{1}{2}$ Convert mixed numbers into fractions: $2\dfrac{1}{4} = \dfrac{2\times4+1}{4} = \dfrac{9}{4}$ and $3\dfrac{1}{2} = \dfrac{3\times2+1}{2} = \dfrac{7}{2}$ Multiply two fractions: $\dfrac{9}{4} \times \dfrac{7}{2} = \dfrac{9\times7}{4\times2} = \dfrac{63}{8}$ The answer is an improper fraction. Convert it into a mixed number: $$\dfrac{63}{8} = 7\dfrac{7}{8}$$
Your Turn!	1) $5\dfrac{2}{3} \times 2\dfrac{2}{9} = 12\dfrac{16}{27}$ 2) $4\dfrac{1}{6} \times 5\dfrac{3}{7} = 22\dfrac{13}{21}$ 3) $3\dfrac{1}{3} \times 3\dfrac{3}{4} = 12\dfrac{1}{2}$ 4) $2\dfrac{2}{9} \times 6\dfrac{1}{3} = 14\dfrac{2}{27}$ 5) $2\dfrac{2}{7} \times 4\dfrac{3}{5} = 10\dfrac{18}{35}$ 6) $1\dfrac{4}{7} \times 9\dfrac{1}{2} = 14\dfrac{13}{14}$ 7) $4\dfrac{1}{8} \times 3\dfrac{2}{3} = 15\dfrac{1}{8}$ 8) $6\dfrac{2}{3} \times 1\dfrac{1}{4} = 8\dfrac{1}{3}$

Name:	Date: ....

Topic	**Dividing Mixed Numbers**
Notes	✓ Convert the mixed numbers into improper fractions. $$a\frac{c}{b} = a + \frac{c}{b} = \frac{ab+c}{b}$$ ✓ Divide fractions and simplify if necessary.
Example	***Solve.*** $2\frac{1}{3} \div 1\frac{1}{4} =$ Converting mixed numbers to fractions: $2\frac{1}{3} \div 1\frac{1}{4} = \frac{7}{3} \div \frac{5}{4}$ Keep, Change, Flip: $\frac{7}{3} \div \frac{5}{4} = \frac{7}{3} \times \frac{4}{5} = \frac{7 \times 4}{3 \times 5} = \frac{28}{15} = 1\frac{13}{15}$
Your Turn!	1) $3\frac{2}{7} \div 2\frac{1}{4} =$ 2) $4\frac{2}{9} \div 1\frac{5}{6} =$ 3) $4\frac{2}{3} \div 3\frac{2}{5} =$ 4) $5\frac{4}{5} \div 4\frac{3}{4} =$ 5) $1\frac{8}{9} \div 2\frac{3}{7} =$ 6) $3\frac{3}{8} \div 2\frac{2}{5} =$ 7) $4\frac{1}{5} \div 3\frac{1}{9} =$ 8) $4\frac{2}{3} \div 1\frac{8}{9} =$ 9) $5\frac{2}{3} \div 3\frac{3}{7} =$ 10) $7\frac{1}{2} \div 5\frac{1}{3} =$

Name: .... **Date:** ....

Topic	Dividing Mixed Numbers- Answers
Notes	✓ Convert the mixed numbers into improper fractions. $$a\frac{c}{b} = a + \frac{c}{b} = \frac{ab+c}{b}$$ ✓ Divide fractions and simplify if necessary.
Example	**Solve.** $2\frac{1}{3} \div 1\frac{1}{4} =$ Converting mixed numbers to fractions: $2\frac{1}{3} \div 1\frac{1}{4} = \frac{7}{3} \div \frac{5}{4}$ Keep, Change, Flip: $\frac{7}{3} \div \frac{5}{4} = \frac{7}{3} \times \frac{4}{5} = \frac{7 \times 4}{3 \times 5} = \frac{28}{15} = 1\frac{13}{15}$
Your Turn!	1) $3\frac{2}{7} \div 2\frac{1}{4} = 1\frac{29}{63}$ 2) $4\frac{2}{9} \div 1\frac{5}{6} = 2\frac{10}{33}$ 3) $4\frac{2}{3} \div 3\frac{2}{5} = 1\frac{19}{51}$ 4) $5\frac{4}{5} \div 4\frac{3}{4} = 1\frac{21}{95}$ 5) $1\frac{8}{9} \div 2\frac{3}{7} = \frac{7}{9}$ 6) $3\frac{3}{8} \div 2\frac{2}{5} = 1\frac{13}{32}$ 7) $4\frac{1}{5} \div 3\frac{1}{9} = 1\frac{7}{20}$ 8) $4\frac{2}{3} \div 1\frac{8}{9} = 2\frac{8}{17}$ 9) $5\frac{2}{3} \div 3\frac{3}{7} = 1\frac{47}{72}$ 10) $7\frac{1}{2} \div 5\frac{1}{3} = 1\frac{13}{32}$

Name:	Date: ....

Topic	**Comparing Decimals**
Notes	Decimals: is a fraction written in a special form. For example, instead of writing $\frac{1}{2}$ you can write **0.5**. For comparing decimals: ✓ Compare each digit of two decimals in the same place value. ✓ Start from left. Compare hundreds, tens, ones, tenth, hundredth, etc. ✓ To compare numbers, use these symbols: - Equal to =, Less than <, Greater than > Greater than or equal ≥, Less than or equal ≤
Examples	***Compare 0.40 and 0.04.*** 0.40 *is greater than* 0.04, because the tenth place of 0.40 is 4, but the tenth place of 0.04 is zero. Then: 0.40 > 0.04 ***Compare 0.0912 and 0.912.*** 0.912 *is greater than* 0.0912, because the tenth place of 0.912 is 9, but the tenth place of 0.0912 is zero. Then: 0.0912 < 0.912
Your Turn!	<table><tr><td>1) 0.91 ☐ 0.95</td><td>2) 1.79 ☐ 1.80</td></tr><tr><td>3) 19.1 ☐ 19.09</td><td>4) 2.45 ☐ 2.089</td></tr><tr><td>5) 1.258 ☐ 12.58</td><td>6) 0.89 ☐ 0.890</td></tr><tr><td>7) 3.871 ☐ 2.998</td><td>8) 0.567 ☐ 0.756</td></tr></table>

Name:	Date: ....

Topic	**Comparing Decimals - Answers**
Notes	Decimals: is a fraction written in a special form. For example, instead of writing $\frac{1}{2}$ you can write **0.5**. For comparing decimals: ✓ Compare each digit of two decimals in the same place value. ✓ Start from left. Compare hundreds, tens, ones, tenth, hundredth, etc. ✓ To compare numbers, use these symbols: - Equal to $=$, Less than $<$, Greater than $>$ Greater than or equal $\geq$, Less than or equal $\leq$
Examples	***Compare 0.40 and 0.04.*** 0.40 *is greater than* 0.04, because the tenth place of 0.40 is 4, but the tenth place of 0.04 is zero. Then: $0.40 > 0.04$ ***Compare 0.0912 and 0.912.*** 0.912 *is greater than* 0.0912, because the tenth place of 0.912 is 9, but the tenth place of 0.0912 is zero. Then: $0.0912 < 0.912$

Your Turn!	1) $0.91 < 0.95$	2) $1.78 < 1.80$
	3) $19.1 > 19.09$	4) $2.45 > 2.089$
	5) $1.258 < 12.58$	6) $0.89 = 0.890$
	7) $3.387 > 2.998$	8) $0.567 < 0.756$

Name:	**Date:** ....

Topic	**Rounding Decimals**
Notes	✓ We can round decimals to a certain accuracy or number of decimal places. ✓ Let's review place values: For example: **35.4817** 3: tens 5: ones 4: tenths 8: hundredths 1: thousandths 7:tens thousandths ✓ To round a decimal, find the place value you'll round to. ✓ Find the digit to the right of the place value you're rounding to. If it is 5 or bigger, add 1 to the place value you're rounding to and remove all digits on its right side. If the digit to the right of the place value is less than 5, keep the place value and remove all digits on the right.
Example	*Round 12.8365 to the hundredth place value.* First look at the next place value to the right, (thousandths). It's 6 and it is greater than 5. Thus add 1 to the digit in the hundredth place. It is 3. → $3 + 1 = 4$, then, the answer is 12.84
Your Turn!	*Round each number to the underlined place value.* 1) 32.5<u>4</u>8 = 2) 2.3<u>2</u>6 = 3) 55.<u>4</u>23 = 4) 2<u>5</u>.62 = 5) 11.<u>2</u>65 = 6) 33.5<u>0</u>5 = 7) 3.5<u>8</u>9 = 8) 8.0<u>1</u>9 =

Name: ....

Date: ....

Topic	**Rounding Decimals - Answers**
Notes	✓ We can round decimals to a certain accuracy or number of decimal places. ✓ Let's review place values: For example: **35.4817** 3: tens 5: ones 4: tenths 8: hundredths 1: thousandths 7: tens thousandths ✓ To round a decimal, find the place value you'll round to. ✓ Find the digit to the right of the place value you're rounding to. If it is 5 or bigger, add 1 to the place value you're rounding to and remove all digits on its right side. If the digit to the right of the place value is less than 5, keep the place value and remove all digits on the right.

Topic	
Example	*Round 12.8365 to the hundredth place value.* First look at the next place value to the right, (thousandths). It's 6 and it is greater than 5. Thus add 1 to the digit in the hundredth place. It is 3. $\rightarrow$ $3 + 1 = 4$, then, the answer is 12.84

Topic		
Your Turn!	*Round each number to the underlined place value.*	
	1) $32.5\underline{4}8 = 32.55$	2) $2.3\underline{2}6 = 2.33$
	3) $55.\underline{4}23 = 55.4$	4) $2\underline{5}.62 = 26$
	5) $11.\underline{2}65 = 11.3$	6) $33.5\underline{0}5 = 33.51$
	7) $3.5\underline{8}9 = 3.59$	8) $8.0\underline{1}9 = 8.02$

Name:	Date: ....

Topic	**Adding and Subtracting Decimals**
Notes	✓ Line up the numbers. ✓ Add zeros to have same number of digits for both numbers if necessary. ✓ Add or subtract using column addition or subtraction.
Examples	**Add**. $2.6 + 5.33 =$ First line up the numbers: $\begin{array}{r} 2.6 \\ + 5.33 \\ \hline \end{array}$ →Add zeros to have same number of digits for both numbers. $\begin{array}{r} 2.60 \\ + 5.33 \\ \hline \end{array}$ → Start with the hundredths place. $0 + 3 = 2,$ $\begin{array}{r} 2.60 \\ + 5.33 \\ \hline 3 \end{array}$ → Continue with tenths place. $6 + 3 = 9,$ $\begin{array}{r} 2.60 \\ + 5.33 \\ \hline .93 \end{array}$ → Add the ones place. $2 + 5 = 7,$ $\begin{array}{r} 2.60 \\ + 5.33 \\ \hline 7.93 \end{array}$ **Subtract**. $4.79 - 3.13 =$ $\begin{array}{r} 4.79 \\ - 3.13 \\ \hline \end{array}$ Start with the hundredths place. $9 - 3 = 6,$ $\begin{array}{r} 4.79 \\ - 3.13 \\ \hline 6 \end{array}$, continue with tenths place. $7 - 1 = 6,$ $\begin{array}{r} 4.79 \\ - 3.13 \\ \hline .66 \end{array}$, subtract the ones place. $4 - 3 = 1,$ $\begin{array}{r} 4.79 \\ - 3.13 \\ \hline 1.66 \end{array}$
Your Turn!	1) $48.13 + 20.15 =$ 2) $78.14 - 65.19 =$ 3) $38.19 + 24.18 =$ 4) $57.26 - 43.54 =$ 5) $27.89 + 46.13 =$ 6) $49.65 - 32.78 =$

Name: ....

Date: ....

Topic	Adding and Subtracting Decimals - Answers
Notes	✓ Line up the numbers. ✓ Add zeros to have same number of digits for both numbers if necessary. ✓ Add or subtract using column addition or subtraction.

Examples

Add. $2.6 + 5.33 =$

First line up the numbers: $\begin{array}{r} 2.6 \\ +5.33 \\ \hline \end{array}$ →Add zeros to have same number of digits

for both numbers. $\begin{array}{r} 2.60 \\ +5.33 \\ \hline \end{array}$ → Start with the hundredths place. $0 + 3 = 2$,

$\begin{array}{r} 2.60 \\ +5.33 \\ \hline 3 \end{array}$ → Continue with tenths place. $6 + 3 = 9$, $\begin{array}{r} 2.60 \\ +5.33 \\ \hline .93 \end{array}$ → Add the ones place.

$2 + 5 = 7$, $\begin{array}{r} 2.60 \\ +5.33 \\ \hline 7.93 \end{array}$

Subtract. $4.79 - 3.13 =$ $\begin{array}{r} 4.79 \\ -3.13 \\ \hline \end{array}$

Start with the hundredths place. $9 - 3 = 6$, $\begin{array}{r} 4.79 \\ -3.13 \\ \hline 6 \end{array}$, continue with tenths

place. $7 - 1 = 6$, $\begin{array}{r} 4.79 \\ -3.13 \\ \hline .66 \end{array}$, subtract the ones place. $4 - 3 = 1$, $\begin{array}{r} 4.79 \\ -3.13 \\ \hline 1.66 \end{array}$

Your Turn!

1) $48.13 + 20.15 = 68.28$	2) $78.14 - 65.19 = 12.95$
3) $38.19 + 24.18 = 62.37$	4) $57.26 - 43.54 = 13.72$
5) $27.89 + 46.13 = 74.02$	6) $49.65 - 32.78 = 16.87$

Name:	**Date:** ....

Topic	**Multiplying and Dividing Decimals**	
Notes	For Multiplication: ✓ Ignore the decimal point and set up and multiply the numbers as you do with whole numbers. ✓ Count the total number of decimal places in both factors. ✓ Place the decimal point in the product. For Division: ✓ If the divisor is not a whole number, move decimal point to right to make it a whole number. Do the same for dividend. ✓ Divide similar to whole numbers.	
Examples	***Find the product.*** $1.2 \times 2.3 =$ Set up and multiply the numbers as you do with whole numbers. Line up the numbers: $\begin{smallmatrix}12\\\times 23\end{smallmatrix} \to$ Multiply: $\frac{\times 23}{276} \to$ Count the total number of decimal places in both of the factors. There are two decimal digits. Then: $1.2 \times 2.3 = 2.76$ ***Find the quotient.*** $5.6 \div 0.8 =$ The divisor is not a whole number. Multiply it by 10 to get 8. $\to 0.8 \times 10 = 8$ Do the same for the dividend to get 56 $\to 5.6 \times 10 = 56$ Now, divide: $56 \div 8 = 7$. The answer is 7.	
Your Turn!	1) $1.13 \times 0.7 =$	2) $48.8 \div 8 =$
	3) $0.9 \times 0.68 =$	4) $66.8 \div 0.2 =$
	5) $0.18 \times 0.5 =$	6) $37.2 \div 100 =$

Name:	Date: ....

Topic	**Multiplying and Dividing Decimals - Answers**	
Notes	For Multiplication: ✓ Ignore the decimal point and set up and multiply the numbers as you do with whole numbers. ✓ Count the total number of decimal places in both factors. ✓ Place the decimal point in the product. For Division: ✓ If the divisor is not a whole number, move decimal point to right to make it a whole number. Do the same for dividend. ✓ Divide similar to whole numbers.	
Examples	***Find the product.*** $1.2 \times 2.3 =$ Set up and multiply the numbers as you do with whole numbers. Line up the numbers: $\begin{array}{r} 12 \\ \times\,23 \\ \hline \end{array}$ → Multiply: $\begin{array}{r} 12 \\ \times\,23 \\ \hline 276 \end{array}$ → Count the total number of decimal places in both of the factors. There are two decimal digits. Then: $1.2 \times 2.3 = 2.76$ ***Find the quotient.*** $5.6 \div 0.8 =$ The divisor is not a whole number. Multiply it by 10 to get 8. → $0.8 \times 10 = 8$ Do the same for the dividend to get 56 → $5.6 \times 10 = 56$ Now, divide: $56 \div 8 = 7$. The answer is 7.	
Your Turn!	1) $1.13 \times 0.7 = 0.791$	2) $48.8 \div 8 = 6.1$
	3) $0.9 \times 0.68 = 0.612$	4) $66.8 \div 0.2 = 334$
	5) $0.18 \times 0.5 = 0.09$	6) $37.2 \div 100 = 0.372$

Name:	Date: ....

Topic	**Adding and Subtracting Integers**
Notes	✓ Integers include: zero, counting numbers, and the negative of the counting numbers. $\{..., -3, -2, -1, 0, 1, 2, 3, ...\}$ ✓ Add a positive integer by moving to the right on the number line. ✓ Add a negative integer by moving to the left on the number line. Subtract an integer by adding its opposite.
Examples	**Solve.** $(4) - (-8) =$ Keep the first number and convert the sign of the second number to its opposite. (change subtraction into addition. Then: $(4) + 8 = 12$ **Solve.** $42 + (12 - 26) =$ First subtract the numbers in brackets, $12 - 26 = -14$ Then: $42 + (-14) = \rightarrow$ change addition into subtraction: $42 - 14 = 28$
Your Turn!	1) $-(15) + 12 =$ 2) $(-2) + (-10) + 18 =$ 3) $(-13) + 7 =$ 4) $3 - (-7) + 14 =$ 5) $(-7) + (-8) =$ 6) $16 - (-4 + 8) =$ 7) $4 + (-15) + 2 =$ 8) $-(22) - (-4) + 8 =$

Name: .... **Date:** ....

Topic	Adding and Subtracting Integers - Answers
Notes	✓ Integers include: zero, counting numbers, and the negative of the counting numbers. $\{ \ldots, -3, -2, -1, 0, 1, 2, 3, \ldots \}$ ✓ Add a positive integer by moving to the right on the number line. ✓ Add a negative integer by moving to the left on the number line. Subtract an integer by adding its opposite.
Examples	***Solve.*** $(4) - (-8) =$ Keep the first number and convert the sign of the second number to its opposite. (change subtraction into addition. Then: $(4) + 8 = 12$ ***Solve.*** $42 + (12 - 26) =$ First subtract the numbers in brackets, $12 - 26 = -14$ Then: $42 + (-14) = \ \rightarrow$ change addition into subtraction: $42 - 14 = 28$

Your Turn!	1) $-(15) + 12 = -3$	2) $(-2) + (-10) + 18 = 6$
	3) $(-13) + 7 = -6$	4) $3 - (-7) + 14 = 24$
	5) $(-7) + (-8) = -15$	6) $16 - (-4 + 8) = 12$
	7) $4 + (-15) + 2 = -9$	8) $(-22) - (-4) + 8 = -10$

Name:	Date: ....

Topic	**Multiplying and Dividing Integers**	
Notes	Use following rules for multiplying and dividing integers: ✓ (negative) × (negative) = positive ✓ (negative) ÷ (negative) = positive ✓ (negative) × (positive) = negative ✓ (negative) ÷ (positive) = negative ✓ (positive) × (positive) = positive ✓ (positive) ÷ (negative) = negative	
Examples	***Solve***. $2 \times (14 - 17) =$ First subtract the numbers in brackets, $14 - 17 = -3 \rightarrow (2) \times (-3) =$ Now use this rule: (positive) × (negative) = negative $(2) \times (-3) = -6$ ***Solve***. $(-7) + (-36 \div 4) =$ First divide -36 by 4, the numbers in brackets, using this rule: (negative) ÷ (positive) = negative Then: $-36 \div 4 = -9$. Now, add -7 and -9: $\qquad (-7) + (-9) = -7 - 9 = -16$	
Your Turn!	1) $(-7) \times 6 =$	2) $(-63) \div (-7) =$
	3) $(-11) \times (-3) =$	4) $81 \div (-9) =$
	5) $(15 - 12) \times (-7) =$	6) $(-12) \div (3) =$
	7) $4 \times (-9) =$	8) $(8) \div (-2) =$

Name:	Date: ....

Topic	**Multiplying and Dividing Integers - Answers**	
Notes	Use following rules for multiplying and dividing integers: ✓ (negative) × (negative) = positive ✓ (negative) ÷ (negative) = positive ✓ (negative) × (positive) = negative ✓ (negative) ÷ (positive) = negative ✓ (positive) × (positive) = positive ✓ (positive) ÷ (negative) = negative	

Examples	***Solve***. $2 \times (14 - 17) =$
	   First subtract the numbers in brackets, $14 - 17 = -3 \rightarrow (2) \times (-3) =$
	   Now use this rule: (positive) × (negative) = negative
	   $(2) \times (-3) = -6$
	
	Solve. $(-7) + (-36 \div 4) =$
	   First divide -36 by 4, the numbers in brackets, using this rule:
	   (negative) ÷ (positive) = negative
	   Then: $-36 \div 4 = -9$. Now, add -7 and -9:
	   $\qquad (-7) + (-9) = -7 - 9 = -16$	

Your Turn!	1) $(-7) \times 6 = -42$	2) $(-63) \div (-7) = 9$
	3) $(-11) \times (-3) = 33$	4) $81 \div (-9) = -9$
	5) $(15 - 12) \times (-7) = -21$	6) $(-12) \div (3) = -4$
	7) $4 \times (-9) = -36$	8) $(8) \div (-2) = -4$

Name:	Date: ....

Topic	Order of Operation
Notes	When there is more than one math operation, use PEMDAS: (to memorize this rule, remember the phrase "Please Excuse My Dear Aunt Sally") ✓ Parentheses ✓ Exponents ✓ Multiplication and Division (from left to right) ✓ Addition and Subtraction (from left to right)
Examples	*Calculate*. $(18 - 26) \div (2^4 \div 4) =$ First simplify inside parentheses: $(-8) \div (16 \div 4) = (-8) \div (4)$ Then: $(-8) \div (4) = -2$ *Solve*. $(-5 \times 7) - (18 - 3^2) =$ First calculate within parentheses: $(-5 \times 7) - (18 - 3^2) = (-35) - (18 - 9)$ Then: $(-35) - (18 - 9) = -35 - 9 = -44$
Your Turn!	1) $(11 \times 4) \div (5 + 6) =$ 3) $(-9) + (5 \times 6) + 14 =$ 5) $[-16(32 \div 2^3)] \div 8 =$ 7) $[16(32 \div 2^3)] - 4^2 =$ 2) $(30 \div 5) + (17 - 8) =$ 4) $(-10 \times 5) \div (2^2 + 1) =$ 6) $(-7) + (72 \div 3^2) + 12 =$ 8) $4^3 + (-5 \times 2^5) + 5 =$

Name:	Date: ....

Topic	**Order of Operation - Answers**
Notes	When there is more than one math operation, use PEMDAS: (to memorize this rule, remember the phrase "Please Excuse My Dear Aunt Sally") ✓ Parentheses ✓ Exponents ✓ Multiplication and Division (from left to right) ✓ Addition and Subtraction (from left to right)
Examples	***Calculate.*** $(18 - 26) \div (2^4 \div 4) =$ First simplify inside parentheses: $(-8) \div (16 \div 4) = (-8) \div (4)$ Then: $(-8) \div (4) = -2$ ***Solve.*** $(-5 \times 7) - (18 - 3^2) =$ First calculate within parentheses: $(-5 \times 7) - (18 - 3^2) = (-35) - (18 - 9)$ Then: $(-35) - (18 - 9) = -35 - 9 = -44$

Your Turn!	1) $(11 \times 4) \div (5 + 6) = 4$	2) $(30 \div 5) + (17 - 8) = 15$
	3) $(-9) + (5 \times 6) + 14 =$ 35	4) $(-10 \times 5) \div (2^2 + 1) = -10$
	5) $[-16(32 \div 2^3)] \div 8 =$ -8	6) $(-7) + (72 \div 3^2) + 12 = 13$
	7) $[16(32 \div 2^3)] - 4^2 =$ 48	8) $4^3 + (-5 \times 2^5) + 5 = -91$

Name: .... | Date: ....

Topic	Integers and Absolute Value
Notes	✓ The absolute value of a number is its distance from zero, in either direction, on the number line. For example, the distance of 9 and -9 from zero on number line is 9. ✓ Absolute value is symbolized by vertical bars, as in $\lvert x \rvert$.
Example	*Calculate.* $\lvert 8-5 \rvert \times \lvert 12-16 \rvert =$ First calculate $\lvert 8-5 \rvert$, $\rightarrow \lvert 8-5 \rvert = \lvert 3 \rvert$, the absolute value of 3 is 3, $\lvert 3 \rvert = 3$ $8 \times \lvert 12-16 \rvert =$ Now calculate $\lvert 12-16 \rvert$, $\rightarrow \lvert 12-16 \rvert = \lvert -4 \rvert$, the absolute value of -4 is 4, $\lvert -4 \rvert = 4$. Then: $3 \times 4 = 12$
Your Turn!	1) $11 - \lvert 4-13 \rvert =$ 2) $14 - \lvert 12-19 \rvert - \lvert 9 \rvert =$ 3) $\lvert 21 \rvert - \dfrac{\lvert -25 \rvert}{5} =$ 4) $\lvert 30 \rvert + \dfrac{\lvert -49 \rvert}{7} =$ 5) $\dfrac{\lvert 7\times -8 \rvert}{4} \times \dfrac{\lvert -12 \rvert}{2} =$ 6) $\dfrac{\lvert 10 \times -6 \rvert}{5} \times \lvert -9 \rvert =$ 7) $\dfrac{\lvert -20 \rvert}{5} \times \dfrac{\lvert -36 \rvert}{6} =$ 8) $\lvert -30+6 \rvert \times \dfrac{\lvert -9\times 4 \rvert}{12} =$

| Name: .... | Date: .... |

Topic	Integers and Absolute Value - Answers
Notes	✓ The absolute value of a number is its distance from zero, in either direction, on the number line. For example, the distance of 9 and -9 from zero on number line is 9. ✓ Absolute value is symbolized by vertical bars, as in $\lvert x \rvert$.
Example	***Calculate.*** $\lvert 8 - 5 \rvert \times \lvert 12 - 16 \rvert =$ First calculate $\lvert 8 - 5 \rvert$, $\rightarrow \lvert 8 - 5 \rvert = \lvert 3 \rvert$, the absolute value of 3 is 3, $\lvert 3 \rvert = 3$ $8 \times \lvert 12 - 16 \rvert =$ Now calculate $\lvert 12 - 16 \rvert$, $\rightarrow \lvert 12 - 16 \rvert = \lvert -4 \rvert$, the absolute value of -4 is 4, $\lvert -4 \rvert = 4$. Then: $3 \times 4 = 12$

Your Turn!		
	1) $11 - \lvert 4 - 13 \rvert = 2$	2) $14 - \lvert 12 - 19 \rvert - \lvert 9 \rvert = -2$
	3) $\lvert 21 \rvert - \dfrac{\lvert -25 \rvert}{5} = 16$	4) $\lvert 30 \rvert + \dfrac{\lvert -49 \rvert}{7} = 37$
	5) $\dfrac{\lvert 7 \times -8 \rvert}{4} \times \dfrac{\lvert -12 \rvert}{2} = 84$	6) $\dfrac{\lvert 10 \times -6 \rvert}{5} \times \lvert -9 \rvert = 108$
	7) $\dfrac{\lvert -20 \rvert}{5} \times \dfrac{\lvert -36 \rvert}{6} = 24$	8) $\lvert -30 + 6 \rvert \times \dfrac{\lvert -9 \times 4 \rvert}{12} = 72$

Name:	Date: ....

Topic	**Simplifying Ratios**
Notes	✓ Ratios are used to make comparisons between two numbers. ✓ Ratios can be written as a fraction, using the word "to", or with a colon. ✓ You can calculate equivalent ratios by multiplying or dividing both sides of the ratio by the same number.
Examples	*Simplify.* $18:63 =$ Both numbers 18 and 63 are divisible by $9 \Rightarrow 18 \div 9 = 2, 63 \div 9 = 7$, Then: $18:63 = 2:7$ *Simplify.* $\frac{25}{45} =$ Both numbers 25 and 45 are divisible by 5, $\Rightarrow 25 \div 5 = 5, 45 \div 5 = 9$, Then: $\frac{25}{45} = \frac{5}{9}$
Your Turn!	1) $\frac{4}{32} = -$ 2) $\frac{25}{80} = -$ 3) $\frac{15}{35} = -$ 4) $\frac{42}{54} = -$ 5) $\frac{12}{36} = -$ 6) $\frac{30}{80} = -$ 7) $\frac{18}{24} = -$ 8) $\frac{60}{108} = -$

| Name: .... | Date: .... |

Topic	**Simplifying Ratios - Answers**
Notes	✓ Ratios are used to make comparisons between two numbers. ✓ Ratios can be written as a fraction, using the word "to", or with a colon. ✓ You can calculate equivalent ratios by multiplying or dividing both sides of the ratio by the same number.
Examples	***Simplify.*** $18:63 =$ Both numbers 18 and 63 are divisible by 9 $\Rightarrow 18 \div 9 = 2, 63 \div 9 = 7$, Then: $18:63 = 2:7$ ***Simplify.*** $\frac{25}{45} =$ Both numbers 25 and 45 are divisible by 5, $\Rightarrow 25 \div 5 = 5, 45 \div 5 = 9$, Then: $\frac{25}{45} = \frac{5}{9}$

Your Turn!		
	1) $\frac{4}{32} = \frac{1}{8}$	2) $\frac{25}{80} = \frac{5}{16}$
	3) $\frac{15}{35} = \frac{3}{7}$	4) $\frac{42}{54} = \frac{7}{9}$
	5) $\frac{12}{36} = \frac{1}{3}$	6) $\frac{30}{80} = \frac{3}{8}$ 7)
	8) $\frac{18}{24} = \frac{3}{4}$	9) $\frac{60}{108} = \frac{5}{9}$

Name:	Date: ....

Topic	**Proportional Ratios**
Notes	✓ Two ratios are proportional if they represent the same relationship. ✓ A proportion means that two ratios are equal. It can be written in two ways: $\frac{a}{b} = \frac{c}{d}$ $\qquad$ $a : b = c : d$
Example	***Solve this proportion for*** x. $\frac{5}{8} = \frac{35}{x}$ Use cross multiplication: $\frac{5}{8} = \frac{35}{x} \Rightarrow 5 \times x = 8 \times 35 \Rightarrow 5x = 280$ Divide to find x: $\quad x = \frac{280}{5} \Rightarrow x = 56$
Your Turn!	1) $\frac{1}{9} = \frac{8}{x} \Rightarrow x =$ _____ $\qquad$ 2) $\frac{5}{8} = \frac{25}{x} \Rightarrow x =$ _____ 3) $\frac{3}{11} = \frac{6}{x} \Rightarrow x =$ _____ $\qquad$ 4) $\frac{12}{20} = \frac{x}{200} \Rightarrow x =$ _____ 5) $\frac{9}{12} = \frac{27}{x} \Rightarrow x =$ _____ $\qquad$ 6) $\frac{14}{16} = \frac{x}{80} \Rightarrow x =$ _____ 7) $\frac{7}{15} = \frac{49}{x} \Rightarrow x =$ _____ $\qquad$ 8) $\frac{8}{19} = \frac{32}{x} \Rightarrow x =$ _____

Name:	Date: ....

Topic	**Proportional Ratios - Answers**
Notes	✓ Two ratios are proportional if they represent the same relationship. ✓ A proportion means that two ratios are equal. It can be written in two ways: $\frac{a}{b} = \frac{c}{d}$ $\qquad a : b = c : d$
Example	***Solve this proportion for*** x. $\frac{5}{8} = \frac{35}{x}$ Use cross multiplication: $\frac{5}{8} = \frac{35}{x} \Rightarrow 5 \times x = 8 \times 35 \Rightarrow 5x = 280$ Divide to find x: $\quad x = \frac{280}{5} \Rightarrow x = 56$

Your Turn!	1) $\frac{1}{9} = \frac{8}{x} \Rightarrow x = 72$	2) $\frac{5}{8} = \frac{25}{x} \Rightarrow x = 40$
	3) $\frac{3}{11} = \frac{6}{x} \Rightarrow x = 22$	4) $\frac{12}{20} = \frac{x}{200} \Rightarrow x = 120$
	5) $\frac{9}{12} = \frac{27}{x} \Rightarrow x = 36$	6) $\frac{14}{16} = \frac{x}{80} \Rightarrow x = 70$
	7) $\frac{7}{15} = \frac{49}{x} \Rightarrow x = 105$	8) $\frac{8}{19} = \frac{32}{x} \Rightarrow x = 76$

Name:	Date: ....

Topic	**Create Proportion**
Notes	✓ To create a proportion, simply find (or create) two equal fractions. ✓ Use cross products to solve proportions or to test whether two ratios are equal and form a proportion. $\frac{a}{b} = \frac{c}{d} \Rightarrow a \times d = c \times b$
Example	*State if this pair of ratios form a proportion.* $\frac{2}{3}$ *and* $\frac{12}{30}$ Use cross multiplication: $\frac{2}{3} = \frac{12}{30} \rightarrow 2 \times 30 = 12 \times 3 \rightarrow 60 = 36$, which is not correct. Therefore, this pair of ratios doesn't form a proportion.

	State if each pair of ratios form a proportion.
Your Turn!	1) $\frac{4}{8}$ *and* $\frac{24}{48}$ 2) $\frac{5}{15}$ *and* $\frac{10}{20}$
	3) $\frac{3}{11}$ *and* $\frac{9}{33}$ 4) $\frac{7}{10}$ *and* $\frac{14}{20}$
	5) $\frac{7}{9}$ *and* $\frac{48}{81}$ 6) $\frac{6}{8}$ *and* $\frac{12}{14}$
	7) $\frac{2}{10}$ *and* $\frac{6}{30}$ 8) $\frac{9}{12}$ *and* $\frac{18}{24}$
	9) Solve. Five pencils costs \$0.65. How many pencils can you buy for \$2.60? _____

Name:	Date: ....

Topic	**Create Proportion**	
Notes	✓ To create a proportion, simply find (or create) two equal fractions. ✓ Use cross products to solve proportions or to test whether two ratios are equal and form a proportion. $\frac{a}{b} = \frac{c}{d} \Rightarrow a \times d = c \times b$	
Example	*State if this pair of ratios form a proportion.* $\frac{2}{3}$ *and* $\frac{12}{30}$ Use cross multiplication: $\frac{2}{3} = \frac{12}{30} \rightarrow 2 \times 30 = 12 \times 3 \rightarrow 60 = 36$, which is not correct. Therefore, this pair of ratios doesn't form a proportion.	
Your Turn!	***State if each pair of ratios form a proportion.***	
	1) $\frac{4}{8}$ *and* $\frac{24}{48}$, *Yes*	2) $\frac{5}{15}$ *and* $\frac{10}{20}$, *No*
	3) $\frac{3}{11}$ *and* $\frac{9}{33}$, *Yes*	4) $\frac{7}{10}$ *and* $\frac{14}{20}$, *Yes*
	5) $\frac{7}{9}$ *and* $\frac{48}{81}$, *No*	6) $\frac{6}{8}$ *and* $\frac{12}{14}$, *No*
	7) $\frac{2}{10}$ *and* $\frac{6}{30}$, *Yes*	8) $\frac{9}{12}$ *and* $\frac{18}{24}$, *Yes*
	9) Solve. Five pencils costs $0.65. How many pencils can you buy for $2.60? 20 pencils	

Name:	Date: ....

Topic	**Similarity and Ratios**	
Notes	✓ Two figures are similar if they have the same shape. ✓ Two or more figures are similar if the corresponding angles are equal, and the corresponding sides are in proportion.	
Example	*Following triangles are similar. What is the value of unknown side?* **Solution:** Find the corresponding sides and write a proportion: $\frac{4}{12} = \frac{x}{9}$. Now, use cross product to solve for x: $\frac{4}{12} = \frac{x}{9} \rightarrow 4 \times 9 = 12 \times x \rightarrow 36 = 12x$. Divide both sides by 12. Then: $5x = 40 \rightarrow \frac{36}{12} = \frac{12x}{12} \rightarrow x = 3$. The missing side is 3.	
Your Turn!	1) 2) 3) 4) 5) 6)	

Name:	Date: ....

Topic	**Similarity and Ratios - Answers**
Notes	✓ Two figures are similar if they have the same shape. ✓ Two or more figures are similar if the corresponding angles are equal, and the corresponding sides are in proportion.
Example	**Following triangles are similar. What is the value of unknown side?** **Solution:** Find the corresponding sides and write a proportion: $\frac{4}{12} = \frac{x}{9}$. Now, use cross product to solve for x: $\frac{4}{12} = \frac{x}{9} \rightarrow 4 \times 9 = 12 \times x \rightarrow 36 = 12x$. Divide both sides by 12. Then: $5x = 40 \rightarrow \frac{36}{12} = \frac{12x}{12} \rightarrow x = 3$. The missing side is 3.
Your Turn!	1) 24 2) 11 3) 4 4) 8 5) 10 6) 9

| Name: .... | Date: .... |

Topic	**Percent Problems**
Notes	✓ In each percent problem, we are looking for the base, or part or the percent. ✓ Use the following equations to find each missing section. ○ Base = Part ÷ Percent ○ Part = Percent × Base ○ Percent = Part ÷ Base
Examples	**18 *is what percent of* 30?** In this problem, we are looking for the percent. Use the following equation: $Percent = Part \div Base \rightarrow Percent = 18 \div 30 = 0.6 = 60\%$ **40 *is* 20% *of what number?*** Use the following formula: $Base = Part \div Percent \rightarrow Base = 40 \div 0.20 = 200$ 40 is 20% of 200.

Your Turn!	1) What is 25 percent of 800?	2) 26 is what percent of 200?
	3) 60 is 5 percent of what number?	4) 48 is what percent of 300?
	5) 84 is 28 percent of what number?	6) 63 is what percent of 700?
	7) 96 is 24 percent of what number?	8) 40 is what percent of 800?

Name:	Date: ....

Topic	**Percent Problems – Answers**	

Notes	✓ In each percent problem, we are looking for the base, or part or the percent.
	 ✓ Use the following equations to find each missing section.
	      ○ Base = Part ÷ Percent
	      ○ Part = Percent × Base
	      ○ Percent = Part ÷ Base	

Examples	**18 *is what percent of* 30?** In this problem, we are looking for the percent. Use the following equation: $$Percent = Part \div Base \rightarrow Percent = 18 \div 30 = 0.6 = 60\%$$ **40 *is* 20% *of what number?*** Use the following formula: $Base = Part \div Percent \rightarrow Base = 40 \div 0.20 = 200$ 40 is 20% of 200.	
Your Turn!	1) What is 25 percent of 800? 200	2) 26 is what percent of 200? 13%
	3) 60 is 5 percent of what number? 1,200	4) 48 is what percent of 300? 16%
	5) 84 is 28 percent of what number? 300	6) 63 is what percent of 700? 9%
	7) 96 is 24 percent of what number? 400	8) 40 is what percent of 800? 5%

Name:	Date: ....

Topic	**Percent of Increase and Decrease**	

Notes	✓ Percent of change (increase or decrease) is a mathematical concept that represents the degree of change over time.
	
	 ✓ To find the percentage of increase or decrease:
	
	    1- New Number – Original Number
	
	    2- The result ÷ Original Number × 100
	
	 Or use this formula: Percent of change = $\frac{new\ number\ -\ original\ number}{original\ number} \times 100$	

Example	The price of a printer increases from $40 to $50. What is the percent increase? **Solution:** Percent of change = $\frac{new\ number\ -\ original\ number}{original\ number} \times 100 = \frac{50\ -\ 40}{40} \times 100 = 25$ The percentage increase is 25. It means that the price of the printer increased 25%.	
Your Turn!	1) In a class, the number of students has been increased from 32 to 36. What is the percentage increase? _____ %	
	2) The price of gasoline rose from $4.50 to $5.40 in one month. By what percent did the gas price rise? _____ %	
	3) A shirt was originally priced at $65.00. It went on sale for $52.00. What was the percent that the shirt was discounted? _____ %	
	4) Jason got a raise, and his hourly wage increased from $40 to $52. What is the percent increase? _____ %	

Name:	Date: ....

Topic	**Percent of Increase and Decrease - Answers**	
Notes	✓ Percent of change (increase or decrease) is a mathematical concept that represents the degree of change over time. ✓ To find the percentage of increase or decrease: 1- New Number – Original Number 2- The result ÷ Original Number × 100 Or use this formula: Percent of change = $\frac{new\ number\ -\ original\ number}{original\ number} \times 100$	
Example	The price of a printer increases from \$40 to \$50. What is the percent increase? **Solution:** Percent of change = $\frac{new\ number\ -\ original\ number}{original\ number} \times 100 = \frac{50-40}{40} \times 100 = 25$ The percentage increase is 25. It means that the price of the printer increased 25%.	
Your Turn!	1) In a class, the number of students has been increased from 32 to 36. What is the percentage increase? 12.5%	
	2) The price of gasoline rose from \$4.50 to \$5.40 in one month. By what percent did the gas price rise? 20%	
	3) A shirt was originally priced at \$65.00. It went on sale for \$52.00. What was the percent that the shirt was discounted? 20%	
	4) Jason got a raise, and his hourly wage increased from \$40 to \$52. What is the percent increase? 30%	

| Name: .... | Date: .... |

Topic	Discount, Tax and Tip

| **Notes** | ✓ Discount = Multiply the regular price by the rate of discount

✓ Selling price = original price – discount

✓ To find tax, multiply the tax rate to the taxable amount (income, property value, etc.)

✓ To find tip, multiply the rate to the selling price. |
| **Example** | The original price of a table is $300 and the tax rate is 6%. What is the final price of the table?

Solution: First find the tax amount. To find tax: Multiply the tax rate to the taxable amount. Tax rate is 6% or 0.06. Then: $0.06 \times 300 = 18$. The tax amount is $18. Final price is: $300 + \$18 = \$318$ |

Your Turn!	1) Original price of a chair: $300 Tax: 15%, Selling price: _____	2) Original price of a computer: $750 Discount: 20%, Selling price: _____
	3) Original price of a printer: $250 Tax: 10%, Selling price: _____	4) Original price of a sofa: $620 Discount: 25%, Selling price: _____
	5) Original price of a mattress: $800 Tax: 12%, Selling price: _____	6) Original price of a book: $150 Discount: 60%, Selling price: _____
	7) Restaurant bill: $35.00 Tip: 20%, Final amount: _____	8) Restaurant bill: $60.00 Tip: 25%, Final amount: _____

| Name: .... | Date: .... |

Topic	**Discount, Tax and Tip - Answers**	
Notes	✓ Discount = Multiply the regular price by the rate of discount ✓ Selling price = original price – discount ✓ To find tax, multiply the tax rate to the taxable amount (income, property value, etc.) ✓ To find tip, multiply the rate to the selling price.	
Example	***The original price of a table is $300 and the tax rate is 6%. What is the final price of the table?*** **Solution:** First find the tax amount. To find tax: Multiply the tax rate to the taxable amount. Tax rate is 6% or 0.06. Then: $0.06 \times 300 = 18$. The tax amount is $18. Final price is: $300 + $18 = $318	
Your Turn!	1) Original price of a chair: $300 Tax: 15%, Selling price: $345	2) Original price of a computer: $750 Discount: 20%, Selling price: $600
	3) Original price of a printer: $250 Tax: 10%, Selling price: $275	4) Original price of a sofa: $620 Discount: 25%, Selling price: $465
	5) Original price of a mattress: $800 Tax: 12%, Selling price: $896	6) Original price of a book: $150 Discount: 60%, Selling price: $60
	7) Restaurant bill: $35.00 Tip: 20%, Final amount: $42	8) Restaurant bill: $60.00 Tip: 25%, Final amount: $75

| Name: .... | Date: .... |

Topic	**Simple Interest**
Notes	✓ Simple Interest: The charge for borrowing money or the return for lending it. To solve a simple interest problem, use this formula: Interest = principal x rate x time $\Rightarrow$ $I = p \times r \times t$
Example	*Find simple interest for* $3,000$ *investment at* 5% *for 4 years.* **Solution:** Use Interest formula: $I = prt$ ($P = \$3,000$, r = $5\% = 0.05$ and $t = 4$) Then: $I = 3,000 \times 0.05 \times 4 = \$600$

Your Turn!	1) $250 at 4% for 3 years. Simple interest: $_____	2) $3,300 at 5% for 6 years. Simple interest: $_____
	3) $720 at 2% for 5 years. Simple interest: $_____	4) $2,200 at 8% for 4 years. Simple interest: $_____
	5) $1,800 at 3% for 2 years. Simple interest: $_____	6) $530 at 4% for 5 years. Simple interest: $_____
	7) $7,000 at 5% for 3 months. Simple interest: $_____	8) $880 at 5% for 9 months. Simple interest: $_____

Name:	**Date:** ....

Topic	Simple Interest - Answers
Notes	✓ Simple Interest: The charge for borrowing money or the return for lending it. To solve a simple interest problem, use this formula: Interest = principal x rate x time $\Rightarrow$ $I = p \times r \times t$
Example	**Find simple interest for** $3,000$ **investment at** 5% **for 4 years.** **Solution:** Use Interest formula: $I = prt$ ($P = \$3,000$, r $= 5\% = 0.05$ and $t = 4$) Then: $I = 3,000 \times 0.05 \times 4 = \$600$
Your Turn!	1) $250 at 4% for 3 years. Simple interest: $30 2) $3,300 at 5% for 6 years. Simple interest: $990 3) $720 at 2% for 5 years. Simple interest: $72 4) $2,200 at 8% for 4 years. Simple interest: $704 5) $1,800 at 3% for 2 years. Simple interest: $108 6) $530 at 4% for 5 years. Simple interest: $106 7) $7,000 at 5% for 3 months. Simple interest: $87.50 8) $880 at 5% for 9 months. Simple interest: $33

Name: ……………………………………..	**Date:** ……………………………………..

Topic	**Simplifying Variable Expressions**
Notes	✓ In algebra, a variable is a letter used to stand for a number. The most common letters are: $x, y, z, a, b, c, m, and\ n$. ✓ Algebraic expression is an expression contains integers, variables, and the math operations such as addition, subtraction, multiplication, division, etc. ✓ In an expression, we can combine "like" terms. (values with same variable and same power)
Example	***Simplify this expression***. $(6x + 8x + 9) =?$ Combine like terms. Then: $(6x + 8x + 4) = 14x + 9$ **(remember you cannot combine variables and numbers).**

Your Turn!	1) $5x + 2 - 2x =$	2) $4 + 7x + 3x =$
	3) $8x + 3 - 3x =$	4) $-2 - x^2 - 6x^2 =$
	5) $3 + 10x^2 + 2 =$	6) $8x^2 + 6x + 7x^2 =$
	7) $5x^2 - 12x^2 + 8x =$	8) $2x^2 - 2x - x + 5x^2 =$
	9) $4x - (12 - 30x) =$	10) $10x - (80x - 48) =$

Name:	Date: ....

Topic	**Simplifying Variable Expressions - Answers**
Notes	✓ In algebra, a variable is a letter used to stand for a number. The most common letters are: $x, y, z, a, b, c, m,$ and n. ✓ Algebraic expression is an expression contains integers, variables, and the math operations such as addition, subtraction, multiplication, division, etc. ✓ In an expression, we can combine "like" terms. (values with same variable and same power)
Example	**Simplify this expression**. $(6x + 8x + 9) = ?$ Combine like terms. Then: $(6x + 8x + 4) = 14x + 9$ *(remember you cannot combine variables and numbers).*

Your Turn!	1) $5x + 2 - 2x =$ $\quad\quad 3x + 2$	2) $4 + 7x + 3x =$ $\quad\quad\quad 10x + 4$
	3) $8x + 3 - 3x =$ $\quad\quad 5x + 3$	4) $-2 - x^2 - 6x^2 =$ $\quad\quad -7x^2 - 2$
	5) $3 + 10x^2 + 2 =$ $\quad\quad 10x^2 + 5$	6) $8x^2 + 6x + 7x^2 =$ $\quad\quad 15x^2 + 6x$
	7) $5x^2 - 12x^2 + 8x =$ $\quad\quad -7x^2 + 8x$	8) $2x^2 - 2x - x + 5x^2 =$ $\quad\quad 72x^2 - 3x$
	9) $4x - (12 - 30x) =$ $\quad\quad 34x - 12$	10) $\quad 10x - (80x - 48) =$ $\quad\quad -70x - 48$

Name: ....   **Date:** ....

Topic	Simplifying Polynomial Expressions
Notes	✓ In mathematics, a polynomial is an expression consisting of variables and coefficients that involves only the operations of addition, subtraction, multiplication, and non–negative integer exponents of variables. $$P(x) = a_n x^n + a_{n-1} x^{n-1} + \ldots + a_2 x^2 + a_1 x + a_0$$
Example	***Simplify this expression.*** $(2x^2 - x^4) - (4x^4 - x^2) =$ First use distributive property: → multiply $(-)$ into $(4x^4 - x^2)$ $(2x^2 - x^4) - (4x^4 - x^2) = 2x^2 - x^4 - 4x^4 + x^2$ Then combine "like" terms: $2x^2 - x^4 - 4x^4 + x^2 = 3x^2 - 5x^4$ And write in standard form: $3x^2 - 5x^4 = -5x^4 + 3x^2$

Your Turn!	1) $(2x^3 + 5x^2) - (12x + 2x^2) =$	2) $(2x^5 + 2x^3) - (7x^3 + 6x^2) =$
	3) $(12x^4 + 4x^2) - (2x^2 - 6x^4) =$	4) $14x - 3x^2 - 2(6x^2 + 6x^3) =$
	5) $(5x^3 - 3) + 5(2x^2 - 3x^3) =$	6) $(4x^3 - 2x) - 2(4x^3 - 2x^4) =$
	7) $2(4x - 3x^3) - 3(3x^3 + 4x^2) =$	8) $(2x^2 - 2x) - (2x^3 + 5x^2) =$

Name:	Date: ....

Topic	**Simplifying Polynomial Expressions - Answers**	
Notes	✓ In mathematics, a polynomial is an expression consisting of variables and coefficients that involves only the operations of addition, subtraction, multiplication, and non–negative integer exponents of variables. $$P(x) = a_n x^n + a_{n-1} x^{n-1} + \ldots + a_2 x^2 + a_1 x + a_0$$	
Example	**Simplify this expression.** $(2x^2 - x^4) - (4x^4 - x^2) =$ First use distributive property: → multiply $(-)$ into $(4x^4 - x^2)$ $(2x^2 - x^4) - (4x^4 - x^2) = 2x^2 - x^4 - 4x^4 + x^2$ Then combine "like" terms: $2x^2 - x^4 - 4x^4 + x^2 = 3x^2 - 5x^4$ And write in standard form: $3x^2 - 5x^4 = -5x^4 + 3x^2$	
Your Turn!	1) $(2x^3 + 5x^2) - (12x + 2x^2) =$ $2x^3 + 3x^2 - 12x$	2) $(2x^5 + 2x^3) - (7x^3 + 6x^2) =$ $2x^5 - 5x^3 - 6x^2$
	3) $(12x^4 + 4x^2) - (2x^2 - 6x^4) =$ $18x^4 + 2x^2$	4) $14x - 3x^2 - 2(6x^2 + 6x^3) =$ $-12x^3 - 15x^2 + 14x$
	5) $(5x^3 - 3) + 5(2x^2 - 3x^3) =$ $-10x^3 + 10x^2 - 3$	6) $(4x^3 - 2x) - 2(4x^3 - 2x^4) =$ $4x^4 - 4x^3 - 2$
	7) $2(4x - 3x^3) - 3(3x^3 + 4x^2) =$ $-15x^3 - 12x^2 + 8x$	8) $(2x^2 - 2x) - (2x^3 + 5x^2) =$ $-2x^3 - 3x^2 - 2x$

Name: ………………………………………….	Date: ……………………………………………

Topic	**Evaluating One Variable**	
Notes	✓ To evaluate one variable expression, find the variable and substitute a number for that variable. ✓ Perform the arithmetic operations.	
Example	*Find the value of this expression for* $x = -3$. $\ -3x - 13$ **Solution:** Substitute -3 for x, then: $-3x - 13 = -3(-3) - 13 = 9 - 13 = -4$	
Your Turn!	1) $x = -3 \Rightarrow 3x + 8 = $ _____	2) $x = 4 \Rightarrow 4(2x + 6) = $ _____
	3) $x = -1 \Rightarrow 6x + 4 = $ _____	4) $x = 7 \Rightarrow 6(5x + 3) = $ _____
	5) $x = 4 \Rightarrow 5(3x + 2) = $ ___	6) $x = 6 \Rightarrow 3(2x + 4) = $ _____
	7) $x = 3 \Rightarrow 7(3x + 1) = $ ___	8) $x = 8 \Rightarrow 3(3x + 7) = $ _____
	9) $x = 9 \Rightarrow 2(x + 9) = $ _____	10) $x = 7 \Rightarrow 2(4x + 5) = $ _____

Name:	Date: ....

Topic	**Evaluating One Variable - Answers**
Notes	✓ To evaluate one variable expression, find the variable and substitute a number for that variable. ✓ Perform the arithmetic operations.
Example	*Find the value of this expression for* $x = -3$. $-3x - 13$ **Solution:** Substitute -3 for x, then: $-3x - 13 = -3(-3) - 13 = 9 - 13 = -4$

Your Turn!	1) $x = -3 \Rightarrow 3x + 8 = -1$	2) $x = 4 \Rightarrow 4(2x + 6) = 56$
	3) $x = -1 \Rightarrow 6x + 4 = -2$	4) $x = 7 \Rightarrow 6(5x + 3) = 228$
	5) $x = 4 \Rightarrow 5(3x + 2) = 70$	6) $x = 6 \Rightarrow 3(2x + 4) = 48$
	7) $x = 3 \Rightarrow 7(3x + 1) = 70$	8) $x = 8 \Rightarrow 3(3x + 7) = 93$
	9) $x = 9 \Rightarrow 2(x + 9) = 36$	10) $x = 7 \Rightarrow 2(4x + 5) = 66$

Name:	Date: ....

Topic	**Evaluating Two Variables**	
Notes	✓ To evaluate an algebraic expression, substitute a number for each variable. ✓ Perform the arithmetic operations to find the value of the expression.	
Example	*Evaluate this expression for* $a = 4$ *and* $b = -2$. $\quad 5a - 6b$ **Solution:** Substitute 4 for a, and -2 for b, then: $\quad 5a - 6b = 5(4) - 6(-2) = 20 + 12 = 32$	
Your Turn!	1) $-4a + 6b$, $a = 4$, $b = 3$ _____	2) $5x + 3y$, $x = 2$, $y = -1$ _____
	3) $-5a + 3b$, $a = 2$, $b = -2$ _____	4) $3x - 4y$, $x = 6$, $y = 2$ _____
	5) $2z + 14 + 6k$, $z = 5$, $\qquad\qquad k = 3$ _____	6) $7a - (9 - 3b)$, $a = 1$, $\qquad\qquad b = 1$ _____
	7) $-6a + 3b$, $a = 4$, $b = 3$ _____	8) $-2a + b$, $a = 6$, $b = 9$ _____
	9) $8x + 2y$, $x = 4$, $y = 5$ _____	10) $z + 4 + 2k$, $z = 7$, $k = 4$ _____

Name:	Date: ....

Topic	**Evaluating Two Variables - Answers**
Notes	✓ To evaluate an algebraic expression, substitute a number for each variable. ✓ Perform the arithmetic operations to find the value of the expression.
Example	*Evaluate this expression for* $a = 4$ *and* $b = -2$. $5a - 6b$ **Solution:** Substitute 4 for a, and -2 for b , then: $5a - 6b = \ 5(4) - 6(-2) = 20 + 12 = 32$

Your Turn!	1) $-4a + 6b, \ a = 4, \ b = 3$
	  2
		2) $5x + 3y, \ x = 2, \ y = -1$
		  7

	3) $-5a + 3b, \ a = 2, \ b = -2$
	  -16
		4) $3x - 4y, \ x = 6, \ y = 2$
		  10

	5) $2z + 14 + 6k, \ z = 5,$
	$\qquad\qquad k = 3$
	  42
		6) $7a - (9 - 3b), \ a = 1,$
		$\qquad\qquad b = 1$
		  1

	7) $-6a + 3b, \ a = 4, \ b = 3$
	  -15
		8) $-2a + b, \ a = 6, \ b = 9$
		  -3

	9) $8x + 2y, \ x = 4, \ y = 5$
	  42
		10) $z + 4 + 2k, \ z = 7, \ k = 4$
		  19

Name:	Date: ....

Topic	**The Distributive Property**	
Notes	✓ The distributive property (or the distributive property of multiplication over addition and subtraction) simplifies and solves expressions in the form of: $a(b + c)$ or $a(b - c)$ ✓ Distributive Property rule: $$a(b + c) = ab + ac$$	
Example	*Simply*. $(5)(2x - 8)$ **Solution:** Use Distributive Property rule: $a(b + c) = ab + ac$ $$(5)(2x - 8) = (5 \times 2x) + (5) \times (-8) = 10x - 40$$	
Your Turn!	1) $(-2)(4 - 3x) =$	2) $(6 - 3x)(-7)$
	3) $6(5 - 9x) =$	4) $10(3 - 5x) =$
	5) $5(6 - 5x) =$	6) $(-2)(-5x + 3) =$
	7) $(8 - 9x)(5) =$	8) $(-16x + 15)(-3) =$
	9) $(-2x + 7)(3) =$	10) $(-18x + 25)(-2) =$

Name:	Date: ....

Topic	**The Distributive Property - Answers**	
Notes	✓ The distributive property (or the distributive property of multiplication over addition and subtraction) simplifies and solves expressions in the form of: $a(b + c)$ or $a(b - c)$ ✓ Distributive Property rule: $$a(b + c) = ab + ac$$	
Example	**Simply.** $(5)(2x - 8)$ **Solution:** Use Distributive Property rule: $a(b + c) = ab + ac$ $$(5)(2x - 8) = (5 \times 2x) + (5) \times (-8) = 10x - 40$$	
Your Turn!	1) $(-2)(4 - 3x) = 6x - 8$	2) $(6 - 3x)(-7) = 21x - 42$
	3) $6(5 - 9x) = -54x + 30$	4) $10(3 - 5x) = -50x + 30$
	5) $5(6 - 5x) = -25x + 30$	6) $(-2)(-5x + 3) = 10x - 6$
	7) $(8 - 9x)(5) = -45x + 40$	8) $(-16x + 15)(-3) =$ $48x - 45$
	9) $(-2x + 7)(3) = -6x + 21$	10) $(-18x + 25)(-2) =$ $36x - 50$

Name:	Date: ....

Topic	**One–Step Equations**

Notes	✓ You only need to perform one Math operation in order to solve the one-step equations.
	 ✓ To solve one-step equation, find the inverse (opposite) operation is being performed.
	 ✓ The inverse operations are:
	    - Addition and subtraction
	    - Multiplication and division

Example	***Solve this equation.*** $x + 42 = 60 \Rightarrow x = ?$ Here, the operation is addition and its inverse operation is subtraction. To solve this equation, subtract 42 from both sides of the *equation:* $x + 42 - 42 = 60 - 42$ Then simplify: $x + 42 - 42 = 60 - 42 \Rightarrow x = 18$

Your Turn!	1) $x - 15 = 36 \Rightarrow x = $ ____	2) $18 = 13 + x \Rightarrow x = $ ____
	3) $x - 22 = 54 \Rightarrow x = $ ____	4) $x + 14 = 24 \Rightarrow x = $ ____
	5) $4x = 24 \Rightarrow x = $ ____	6) $\frac{x}{6} = -3 \Rightarrow x = $ ____
	7) $99 = 11x \Rightarrow x = $ ____	8) $\frac{x}{12} = 6 \Rightarrow x = $ ____

Name:	Date: ....

Topic	One–Step Equations - Answers

Notes	✓ You only need to perform one Math operation in order to solve the one-step equations.
	✓ To solve one-step equation, find the inverse (opposite) operation is being performed.
	✓ The inverse operations are:
	    - Addition and subtraction
	    - Multiplication and division

Example	***Solve this equation.*** $\ x + 42 = 60 \Rightarrow x = ?$ Here, the operation is addition and its inverse operation is subtraction. To solve this equation, subtract 42 from both sides of the *equation:* $x + 42 - 42 = 60 - 42$ Then simplify: $x + 42 - 42 = 60 - 42 \Rightarrow x = 18$
Your Turn!	1) $x - 15 = 36 \Rightarrow x = 51$ 2) $18 = 13 + x \Rightarrow x = 5$ 3) $x - 22 = 54 \Rightarrow x = 76$ 4) $x + 14 = 24 \Rightarrow x = 10$ 5) $4x = 24 \Rightarrow x = 6$ 6) $\frac{x}{6} = -3 \Rightarrow x = -18$ 7) $99 = 11x \Rightarrow x = 9$ 8) $\frac{x}{12} = 6 \Rightarrow x = 72$

Name:	Date: ....

Topic	Multi –Step Equations - Answers
Notes	✓ Combine "like" terms on one side. ✓ Bring variables to one side by adding or subtracting. ✓ Simplify using the inverse of addition or subtraction. ✓ Simplify further by using the inverse of multiplication or division. ✓ Check your solution by plugging the value of the variable into the original equation.
Example	*Solve this equation for x.* $2x - 3 = 13$ **Solution:** The inverse of subtraction is addition. Add 3 to both sides of the equation. Then: $2x - 3 = 13 \Rightarrow 2x - 3 = 13 + 3$ $\Rightarrow 2x = 16$. Now, divide both sides by 2, then: $\frac{2x}{2} = \frac{16}{2} \Rightarrow x = 8$ Now, check the solution: $x = 8 \Rightarrow 2x - 3 = 13 \Rightarrow 2(8) - 3 = 13 \Rightarrow 16 - 3 = 13$ The answer $x = 8$ is correct.
Your Turn!	1) $4x - 12 = 8 \Rightarrow x =$ 2) $12 - 3x = -6 + 3x \Rightarrow x =$ 3) $3(4 - 2x) = 24 \Rightarrow x =$ 4) $15 + 5x = -7 - 6x \Rightarrow x =$ 5) $-2(5 + x) = 2 \Rightarrow x =$ 6) $12 - 2x = -3 - 5x \Rightarrow x =$ 7) $14 = -(x - 9) \Rightarrow x =$ 8) $11 - 4x = -4 - 3x \Rightarrow x =$

Name:	Date: ....

Topic	**Multi –Step Equations - Answers**	
Notes	✓ Combine "like" terms on one side. ✓ Bring variables to one side by adding or subtracting. ✓ Simplify using the inverse of addition or subtraction. ✓ Simplify further by using the inverse of multiplication or division. ✓ Check your solution by plugging the value of the variable into the original equation.	
Example	*Solve this equation for* x. $2x - 3 = 13$ **Solution:** The inverse of subtraction is addition. Add 3 to both sides of the equation. Then: $2x - 3 = 13 \Rightarrow 2x - 3 = 13 + 3$ $\Rightarrow 2x = 16$. Now, divide both sides by 2, then: $\frac{2x}{2} = \frac{16}{2} \Rightarrow x = 8$ Now, check the solution: $x = 8 \Rightarrow 2x - 3 = 13 \Rightarrow 2(8) - 3 = 13 \Rightarrow 16 - 3 = 13$ The answer $x = 8$ is correct.	
Your Turn!	1) $4x - 12 = 8 \Rightarrow x = 5$	2) $12 - 3x = -6 + 3x \Rightarrow x = 3$
	3) $3(4 - 2x) = 24 \Rightarrow x = -2$	4) $15 + 5x = -7 - 6x \Rightarrow x = -2$
	5) $-2(5 + x) = 2 \Rightarrow x = -6$	6) $12 - 2x = -3 - 5x \Rightarrow x = -5$
	7) $14 = -(x - 9) \Rightarrow x = -5$	8) $11 - 4x = -4 - 3x \Rightarrow x = 15$

Name:	**Date:** ....

Topic	**System of Equations**
Notes	✓ A system of equations contains two equations and two variables. For example, consider the system of equations: $x - 2y = -2, x + 2y = 10$ ✓ The easiest way to solve a system of equation is using the elimination method. The elimination method uses the addition property of equality. You can add the same value to each side of an equation. ✓ For the first equation above, you can add $x + 2y$ to the left side and 10 to the right side of the first equation: $x - 2y + (x + 2y) = -2 + 10$. Now, if you simplify, you get: $x - 2y + (x + 2y) = -2 + 10 \rightarrow 2x = 8 \rightarrow x = 4$. Now, substitute 4 for the x in the first equation: $4 - 2y = -2$. By solving this equation, $y = 3$
Example	What is the value of x and y in this system of equations? $\begin{cases} 3x - y = 7 \\ -x + 4y = 5 \end{cases}$ **Solution:** Solving System of Equations by Elimination: $\begin{array}{r} 3x - y = 7 \\ \underline{-x + 4y = 5} \end{array}$ Multiply the second equation by 3, then add it to the first equation. $\begin{array}{r} 3x - y = 7 \\ \underline{3(-x + 4y = 5)} \end{array} \Rightarrow \begin{array}{r} 3x - y = 7 \\ -3x + 12y = 15) \end{array} \Rightarrow 11y = 22 \Rightarrow y = 2$. Now, substitute 2 for y in the first equation and solve for x. $3x - (2) = 7 \Rightarrow 3x = 9 \Rightarrow x = 3$

Your Turn!	1) $-4x + 4y = 8$ $-4x + 2y = 6$	2) $-5x + y = -3$ $3x - 8y = 24$
	$x =$ ____ $y =$ ____	$x =$ ____ $y =$ ____
	3) $y = -2$ $4x - 3y = 8$	4) $y = -3x + 5$ $5x - 4y = -3$
	$x =$ ____ $y =$ ____	$x =$ ____ $y =$ ____
	5) $20x - 18y = -26$ $-10x + 6y = 22$	6) $-9x - 12y = 15$ $2x - 6y = 14$
	$x =$ ____ $y =$ ____	$x =$ ____ $y =$ ____

Name:	Date: ....

Topic	System of Equations- Answers
Notes	✓ A system of equations contains two equations and two variables. For example, consider the system of equations: $x - 2y = -2, x + 2y = 10$ ✓ The easiest way to solve a system of equation is using the elimination method. The elimination method uses the addition property of equality. You can add the same value to each side of an equation. ✓ For the first equation above, you can add $x + 2y$ to the left side and 10 to the right side of the first equation: $x - 2y + (x + 2y) = -2 + 10$. Now, if you simplify, you get: $x - 2y + (x + 2y) = -2 + 10 \rightarrow 2x = 8 \rightarrow x = 4$. Now, substitute 4 for the x in the first equation: $4 - 2y = -2$. By solving this equation, $y = 3$
Example	What is the value of x and y in this system of equations? $\begin{cases} 3x - y = 7 \\ -x + 4y = 5 \end{cases}$ **Solution:** Solving System of Equations by Elimination: $\begin{array}{l} 3x - y = 7 \\ \underline{-x + 4y = 5} \end{array}$ Multiply the second equation by 3, then add it to the first equation. $\begin{array}{l} 3x - y = 7 \\ \underline{3(-x + 4y = 5)} \end{array} \Rightarrow \begin{array}{l} 3x - y = 7 \\ \underline{-3x + 12y = 15)} \end{array} \Rightarrow 11y = 22 \Rightarrow y = 2$. Now, substitute 2 for y in the first equation and solve for x. $3x - (2) = 7 \Rightarrow 3x = 9 \Rightarrow x = 3$
Your Turn!	1) $-4x + 4y = 8$ $-4x + 2y = 6$ 2) $-5x + y = -3$ $3x - 8y = 24$

1) $-4x + 4y = 8$ $-4x + 2y = 6$	2) $-5x + y = -3$ $3x - 8y = 24$
$x = -1$ $y = 1$	$x = 0$ $y = -3$
3) $y = -2$ $4x - 3y = 8$	4) $y = -3x + 5$ $5x - 4y = -3$
$x = \dfrac{1}{2}$ $y = -2$	$x = 1$ $y = 2$
5) $20x - 18y = -26$ $-10x + 6y = 22$	6) $-9x - 12y = 15$ $2x - 6y = 14$
$x = -4$ $y = -3$	$x = 1$ $y = -2$

Name: .... **Date:** ....

Topic: **Graphing Single–Variable Inequalities**

Notes

- ✓ An inequality compares two expressions using an inequality sign.
- ✓ Inequality signs are: "less than" $<$, "greater than" $>$, "less than or equal to" $\leq$, and "greater than or equal to" $\geq$.
- ✓ To graph a single–variable inequality, find the value of the inequality on the number line.
- ✓ For less than ($<$) or greater than ($>$) draw open circle on the value of the variable. If there is an equal sign too, then use filled circle.
- ✓ Draw an arrow to the right for greater or to the left for less than.

Example

Draw a graph for this inequality. $x < 5$

Solution: Since, the variable is less than 5, then we need to find 5 in the number lin and draw an open circle on it. Then, draw an arrow to the left.

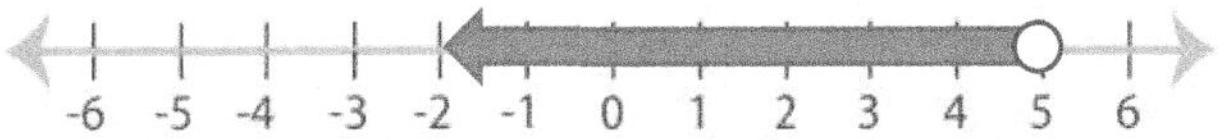

Your Turn!

1) $x < 4$

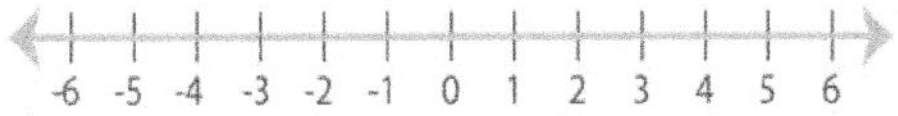

2) $x \geq -1$

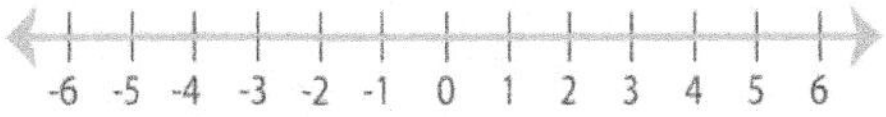

3) $x \geq -3$

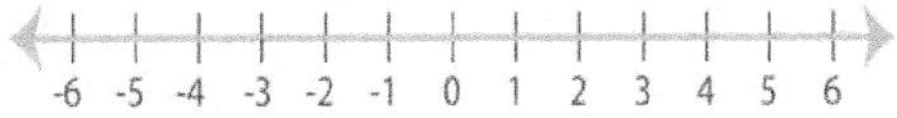

4) $x \leq 6$

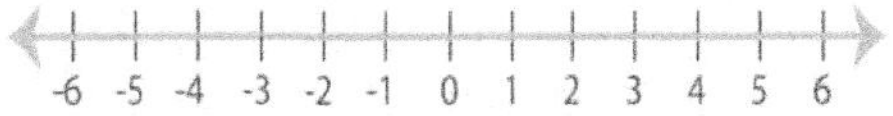

5) $x > -6$

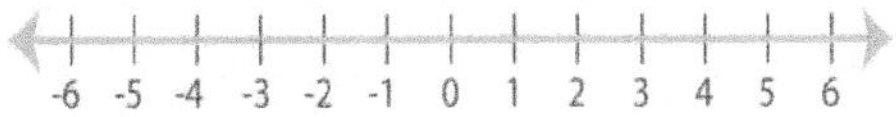

6) $2 > x$

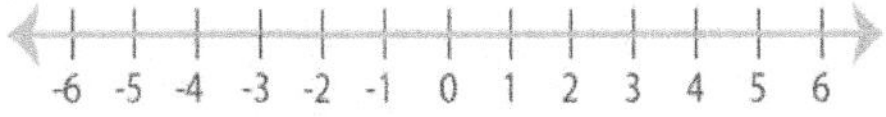

7) $-2 \leq x$

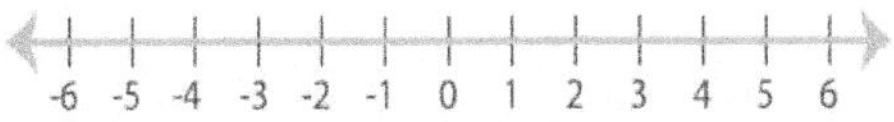

8) $x > 0$

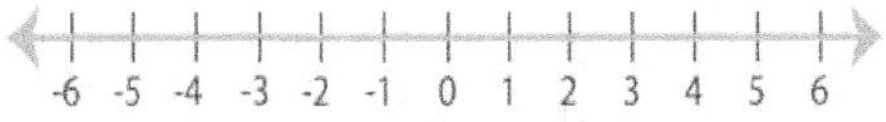

Name:	Date: ....

Topic	**Graphing Single–Variable Inequalities- Answers**
Notes	✓ An inequality compares two expressions using an inequality sign. ✓ Inequality signs are: "less than" <, "greater than" >, "less than or equal to" ≤, and "greater than or equal to" ≥. ✓ To graph a single–variable inequality, find the value of the inequality on the number line. ✓ For less than (<) or greater than (>) draw open circle on the value of the variable. If there is an equal sign too, then use filled circle. ✓ Draw an arrow to the right for greater or to the left for less than.
Example	**Draw a graph for this inequality .** $x < 5$ **Solution:** Since, the variable is less than 5, then we need to find 5 in the number line and draw an open circle on it. Then, draw an arrow to the left.

Your Turn!	1) $x < 4$	2) $x \geq -1$
	3) $x \geq -3$	4) $x \leq 6$
	5) $x > -6$	6) $2 > x$
	7) $-2 \leq x$	8) $x > 0$

Name:	Date: ....

Topic	One–Step Inequalities
Notes	✓ Inequality signs are: "less than" $<$, "greater than" $>$, "less than or equal to" $\leq$, and "greater than or equal to" $\geq$. ✓ You only need to perform one Math operation in order to solve the one-step inequalities. ✓ To solve one-step inequalities, find the inverse (opposite) operation is being performed. ✓ For dividing or multiplying both sides by negative numbers, flip the direction of the inequality sign.
Example	***Solve this inequality.*** $\quad x + 12 < 60 \Rightarrow$ _____ Here, the operation is addition and its inverse operation is subtraction. To solve this inequality, subtract 12 from both sides of the ***inequality:*** $x + 12 - 12 < 60 - 12$ Then simplify: $x < 48$

Your Turn!	1) $4x < -8 \Rightarrow$ _____	2) $x + 6 > 28 \Rightarrow$ _____
	3) $-3x \geq 36 \Rightarrow$ _____	4) $x - 16 \leq 4 \Rightarrow$ _____
	5) $\frac{x}{2} \geq -9 \Rightarrow$ _____	6) $48 < 6x \Rightarrow$ _____
	7) $77 \leq 11x \Rightarrow$ _____	8) $\frac{x}{4} > 9 \Rightarrow$ _____

| Name: .... | Date: .... |

Topic	One–Step Inequalities - Answers
Notes	✓ Inequality signs are: "less than" <, "greater than" >, "less than or equal to" ≤, and "greater than or equal to" ≥. ✓ You only need to perform one Math operation in order to solve the one-step inequalities. ✓ To solve one-step inequalities, find the inverse (opposite) operation is being performed. ✓ For dividing or multiplying both sides by negative numbers, flip the direction of the inequality sign.
Example	**Solve this inequality.** $x + 12 < 60 \Rightarrow$ _____ Here, the operation is addition and its inverse operation is subtraction. To solve this inequality, subtract 12 from both sides of the ***inequality:*** $x + 12 - 12 < 60 - 12$ Then simplify: $x < 48$
Your Turn!	1) $4x < -8 \Rightarrow x < -2$ 2) $x + 6 > 28 \Rightarrow x > 22$ 3) $-3x \geq 36 \Rightarrow x \leq -12$ 4) $x - 16 \leq 4 \Rightarrow x \leq 20$ 5) $\frac{x}{2} \geq -9 \Rightarrow x \geq -18$ 6) $48 < 6x \Rightarrow 8 < x$ 7) $77 \leq 11x \Rightarrow 7 \leq x$ 8) $\frac{x}{4} > 9 \Rightarrow x > 36$

Name:	Date: ....

Topic	**Multi –Step Inequalities**	
Notes	✓ Isolate the variable. ✓ Simplify using the inverse of addition or subtraction. ✓ Simplify further by using the inverse of multiplication or division. ✓ For dividing or multiplying both sides by negative numbers, flip the direction of the inequality sign.	
Example	***Solve this inequality.*** $3x + 12 \leq 21$ **Solution:** First subtract 12 from both sides: $3x + 12 - 12 \leq 21 - 12$ Then simplify: $3x + 12 - 12 \leq 21 - 12 \rightarrow 3x \leq 9$ Now divide both sides by 3: $\frac{3x}{3} \leq \frac{9}{3} \rightarrow x \leq 3$	
Your Turn!	1) $5x + 6 < 36 \rightarrow$ _____	2) $2x - 8 \leq 6 \rightarrow$ _____
	3) $2x - 5 \leq 17 \rightarrow$ _____	4) $14 - 7x \geq -7 \rightarrow$ _____
	5) $18 - 6x \geq -6 \rightarrow$ _____	6) $2x - 18 \leq 16 \rightarrow$ _____
	7) $8 + 4x < 44 \rightarrow$ _____	8) $5 - 4x < 17 \rightarrow$ _____

| Name: .... | Date: .... |

Topic	Multi –Step Inequalities - Answers
Notes	✓ Isolate the variable. ✓ Simplify using the inverse of addition or subtraction. ✓ Simplify further by using the inverse of multiplication or division. ✓ For dividing or multiplying both sides by negative numbers, flip the direction of the inequality sign.
Example	*Solve this inequality*. $3x + 12 \leq 21$ **Solution:** First subtract 12 from both sides: $3x + 12 - 12 \leq 21 - 12$ Then simplify: $3x + 12 - 12 \leq 21 - 12 \rightarrow 3x \leq 9$ Now divide both sides by 3: $\frac{3x}{3} \leq \frac{9}{3} \rightarrow x \leq 3$

Your Turn!

1) $5x + 6 < 36 \rightarrow x < 6$

2) $2x - 8 \leq 6 \rightarrow x \leq 7$

3) $2x - 5 \leq 17 \rightarrow x \leq 11$

4) $14 - 7x \geq -7 \rightarrow x \leq 3$

5) $18 - 6x \geq -6 \rightarrow x \leq 4$

6) $2x - 18 \leq 16 \rightarrow x \leq 17$

7) $8 + 4x < 44 \rightarrow x < 9$

8) $5 - 4x < 17 \rightarrow x > -3$

Name:	Date: ....

Topic	**Finding Slope**	
Notes	<ul><li>The slope of a line represents the direction of a line on the coordinate plane.</li><li>A line on coordinate plane can be drawn by connecting two points.</li><li>To find the slope of a line, we need two points.</li><li>The slope of a line with two points A (x_1, y_1) and B (x_2, y_2) can be found by using this formula: $\frac{y_2 - y_1}{x_2 - x_1} = \frac{rise}{run}$</li><li>The equation of a line is typically written as $y = mx + b$ where m is the slope and b is the y-intercept.</li></ul>	
Examples	***Find the slope of the line through these two points:*** $(4, -12)$ *and* $(9, 8)$. **Solution:** Slope $= \frac{y_2 - y_1}{x_2 - x_1}$. Let (x_1, y_1) be $(4, -12)$ and (x_2, y_2) be $(9, 8)$. ***Then:*** slope $= \frac{y_2 - y_1}{x_2 - x_1} = \frac{8 - (-12)}{9 - 4} = \frac{8 + 12}{5} = \frac{20}{5} = 4$ ***Find the slope of the line with equation*** $y = 5x - 6$ **Solution:** when the equation of a line is written in the form of $y = mx + b$, the slope is m. In this line: $y = 5x - 6$, the slope is 5.	

Your Turn!	1) $(2, 3), (4, 7)$
	
	   Slope = ____
		2) $(-2, 2), (0, 4)$
		
		   Slope = ____

	3) $(4, -2), (2, 4)$
	
	   Slope = ____
		4) $(-4, -1), (0, 7)$
		
		   Slope = ____

	5) $y = 3x + 18$
	
	   Slope = ____
		6) $y = 12x - 3$
		
		   Slope = ____

| Name: .... | Date: .... |

Topic	**Finding Slope - Answers**
Notes	✓ The slope of a line represents the direction of a line on the coordinate plane. ✓ A line on coordinate plane can be drawn by connecting two points. ✓ To find the slope of a line, we need two points. ✓ The slope of a line with two points A (x_1, y_1) and B (x_2, y_2) can be found by using this formula: $\frac{y_2 - y_1}{x_2 - x_1} = \frac{rise}{run}$ ✓ The equation of a line is typically written as $y = mx + b$ where m is the slope and b is the y-intercept.
Examples	*Find the slope of the line through these two points:* $(4, -12)\ and\ (9, 8)$. **Solution:** Slope $= \frac{y_2 - y_1}{x_2 - x_1}$. Let (x_1, y_1) be $(4, -12)$ and (x_2, y_2) be $(9, 8)$. **Then:** slope $= \frac{y_2 - y_1}{x_2 - x_1} = \frac{8 - (-12)}{9 - 4} = \frac{8 + 12}{5} = \frac{20}{5} = 4$ *Find the slope of the line with equation* $y = 5x - 6$ **Solution:** when the equation of a line is written in the form of $y = mx + b$, the slope is m. In this line: $y = 5x - 6$, the slope is 5.
Your Turn!	1) $(2, 3), (4, 7)$ Slope $= 2$ 2) $(-2, 2), (0, 4)$ Slope $= 1$ 3) $(4, -2), (2, 4)$ Slope $= -3$ 4) $(-4, -1), (0, 7)$ Slope $= 2$ 5) $y = 3x + 18$ Slope $= 3$ 6) $y = 12x - 3$ Slope $= 12$

Name:	**Date:** ....

Topic	**Graphing Lines Using Slope–Intercept Form**
Notes	✓ Slope–intercept form of a line: given the slope m and the y–intercept (the intersection of the line and y-axis) b, then the equation of the line is: $$y = mx + b$$
Example	***Sketch the graph of*** $y = -2x - 1$**.** **Solution:** To graph this line, we need to find two points. When x is zero the value of y is -1. And when y is zero the value of x is $-\frac{1}{2}$. $$x = 0 \rightarrow y = -2(0) - 1 = -1, y = 0 \rightarrow 0$$ $$= -2x - 1 \rightarrow x = -\frac{1}{2}$$ Now, we have two points: $(0, -1)$ and $(-\frac{1}{2}, 0)$. Find the points and graph the line. Remember that the slope of the line is $-\frac{1}{2}$. 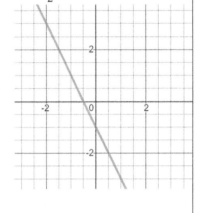
Your Turn!	1) $y = -4x + 1$ 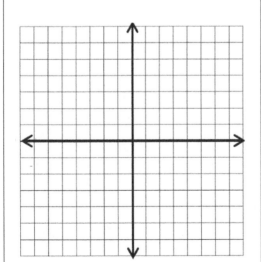 2) $y = -x - 5$ 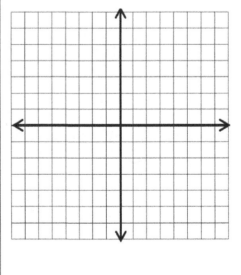

Name:	Date: ....:.............................

Topic	**Graphing Lines Using Slope–Intercept Form - Answers**
Notes	✓ Slope–intercept form of a line: given the slope m and the y–intercept (the intersection of the line and y-axis) b, then the equation of the line is: $$y = mx + b$$
Example	*Sketch the graph of* $y = -2x - 1$. **Solution:** To graph this line, we need to find two points. When x is zero the value of y is -1. And when y is zero the value of x is $-\frac{1}{2}$. $$x = 0 \rightarrow y = -2(0) - 1 = -1, y = 0 \rightarrow 0$$ $$= -2x - 1 \rightarrow x = -\frac{1}{2}$$ Now, we have two points: $(0, -1)$ and $(-\frac{1}{2}, 0)$. Find the points and graph the line. Remember that the slope of the line is $-\frac{1}{2}$.
Your Turn!	1) $y = -4x + 1$ 2) $y = -x - 5$

Name:	Date: ....

Topic	**Writing Linear Equations**
Notes	✓ The equation of a line: $y = mx + b$ ✓ Identify the slope. ✓ Find the y–intercept. This can be done by substituting the slope and the coordinates of a point (x, y) on the line.
Example	**Write the equation of the line through $(3, 1)$ and $(-1, 5)$.** **Solution:** $Slop = \frac{y_2 - y_1}{x_2 - x_1} = \frac{5 - 1}{-1 - 3} = \frac{4}{-4} = -1 \rightarrow m = -1$ To find the value of b, you can use either points. The answer will be the same: $y = -x + b$ $(3, 1) \rightarrow 1 = -3 + b \rightarrow b = 4$ $(-1, 5) \rightarrow 5 = -(-1) + b \rightarrow b = 4$ The equation of the line is: $y = -x + 4$

Your Turn!	1) through: $(-2, 7), (1, 4)$ $y =$	2) through: $(6, 1), (5, 2)$ $y =$
	3) through: $(5, -1), (8, 2)$ $y =$	4) through: $(-2, 4), (4, -8)$ $y =$
	5) through: $(6, -5), (-5, 6)$ $y =$	6) through: $(4, -4), (-2, 8)$ $y =$
	7) through $(8, 8)$, Slope: 2 $y =$	8) through $(-7, 10)$, Slope: -2 $y =$

Name:	Date: ....

Topic	Writing Linear Equations - Answers	
Notes	✓ The equation of a line: $y = mx + b$ ✓ Identify the slope. ✓ Find the y–intercept. This can be done by substituting the slope and the coordinates of a point (x, y) on the line.	
Example	**Write the equation of the line through $(3, 1)$ and $(-1, 5)$.** **Solution:** $Slop = \frac{y_2 - y_1}{x_2 - x_1} = \frac{5-1}{-1-3} = \frac{4}{-4} = -1 \rightarrow m = -1$ To find the value of b, you can use either points. The answer will be the same: $y = -x + b$ $(3, 1) \rightarrow 1 = -3 + b \rightarrow b = 4$ $(-1, 5) \rightarrow 5 = -(-1) + b \rightarrow b = 4$ The equation of the line is: $y = -x + 4$	
Your Turn!	1) through: $(-2, 7), (1, 4)$ $y = -x + 5$	2) through: $(6, 1), (5, 2)$ $y = -x + 7$
	3) through: $(5, -1), (8, 2)$ $y = x - 6$	4) through: $(-2, 4), (4, -8)$ $y = -2x$
	5) through: $(6, -5), (-5, 6)$ $y = -x + 1$	6) through: $(4, -4), (-2, 8)$ $y = -2x + 4$
	7) through $(8, 8)$, Slope: 2 $y = 2x - 8$	8) through $(-7, 10)$, Slope: -2 $y = -2x - 4$

Name:	Date: ....

Topic	**Finding Midpoint**
Notes	✓ The middle of a line segment is its midpoint. ✓ The Midpoint of two endpoints A (x_1, y_1) and B (x_2, y_2) can be found using this formula: $M(\frac{x_1+x_2}{2}, \frac{y_1+y_2}{2})$
Example	Find the midpoint of the line segment with the given endpoints. $(\mathbf{1}, -\mathbf{2}), (\mathbf{3}, \mathbf{6})$ **Solution:** Midpoint $= (\frac{x_1+x_2}{2}, \frac{y_1+y_2}{2}) \rightarrow (x_1, y_1) = (1, -2)$ and $(x_2, y_2) = (3, 6)$ Midpoint $= (\frac{1+3}{2}, \frac{-2+6}{2}) \rightarrow (\frac{4}{2}, \frac{4}{2}) \rightarrow M(2, 2)$

Your Turn!	1) $(6, 0), (-4, 2)$
	
	     Midpoint = (__, __)
	
	 3) $(-3, 4), (-5, 0)$
	
	     Midpoint = (__, __)
	
	 5) $(6, 7), (-4, 5)$
	
	     Midpoint = (__, __)
	
	 7) $(7, 3), (-1, -7)$
	
	     Midpoint = (__, __)
	
	 9) $(3, 4), (-7, -6)$
	
	     Midpoint = (__, __)
	
	 2) $(4, -1), (2, 3)$
	
	     Midpoint = (__, __)
	
	 4) $(8, 1), (-4, 5)$
	
	     Midpoint = (__, __)
	
	 6) $(2, -3), (2, 5)$
	
	     Midpoint = (__, __)
	
	 8) $(3, 9), (-1, 5)$
	
	     Midpoint = (__, __)
	
	 10) $(-5, 2), (11, -6)$
	
	     Midpoint = (__, __)

Name:	Date: ....

Topic	**Finding Midpoint - Answers**
Notes	✓ The middle of a line segment is its midpoint. ✓ The Midpoint of two endpoints A (x_1, y_1) and B (x_2, y_2) can be found using this formula: $M(\frac{x_1+x_2}{2}, \frac{y_1+y_2}{2})$
Example	Find the midpoint of the line segment with the given endpoints. $(\mathbf{1}, -\mathbf{2}), (\mathbf{3}, \mathbf{6})$ **Solution:** Midpoint $= (\frac{x_1+x_2}{2}, \frac{y_1+y_2}{2}) \rightarrow (x_1, y_1) = (1, -2)$ and $(x_2, y_2) = (3, 6)$ Midpoint $= (\frac{1+3}{2}, \frac{-2+6}{2}) \rightarrow (\frac{4}{2}, \frac{4}{2}) \rightarrow M(2, 2)$

Your Turn!	1) $(6, 0), (-4, 2)$ **Midpoint** $= (1, 1)$	2) $(4, -1), (2, 3)$ **Midpoint** $= (3, 1)$
	3) $(-3, 4), (-5, 0)$ **Midpoint** $= (-4, 2)$	4) $(8, 1), (-4, 5)$ **Midpoint** $= (2, 3)$
	5) $(6, 7), (-4, 5)$ **Midpoint** $= (1, 6)$	6) $(2, -3), (2, 5)$ **Midpoint** $= (2, 1)$
	7) $(7, 3), (-1, -7)$ **Midpoint** $= (3, -2)$	8) $(3, 9), (-1, 5)$ **Midpoint** $= (1, 7)$
	9) $(3, 4), (-7, -6)$ **Midpoint** $= (-2, -1)$	10) $(-5, 2), (11, -6)$ **Midpoint** $= (3, -2)$

Name:	Date: ....

Topic	**Finding Distance of Two Points**
Notes	✓ Use this formula to find the distance of two points A (x_1, y_1) and B (x_2, y_2): $$d = \sqrt{(x_2 - x_1)^2 + (y_2 - y_1)^2}$$
Example	**Find the distance of two points** $(-1, 5)$ and $(4, -7)$. Solution: **Use distance of two points formula:** $d = \sqrt{(x_2 - x_1)^2 + (y_2 - y_1)^2}$ $(x_1, y_1) = (-1, 5)$, and $(x_2, y_2) = (4, -7)$ Then: $d = \sqrt{(x_2 - x_1)^2 + (y_2 - y_1)^2} \rightarrow d =$ $\sqrt{(4 - (-1))^2 + (-7 - 5)^2} = \sqrt{(-5)^2 + (-12)^2} = \sqrt{25 + 144} =$ $\sqrt{169} = 13$

Your Turn!	1) $(6, 2), (-4, 2)$ Distance = ____	2) $(2, -3), (2, 5)$ Distance = ____
	3) $(-5, 10), (7, 1)$ Distance = ____	4) $(8, 1), (-4, 6)$ Distance = ____
	5) $(-3, 6), (-4, 5)$ Distance = ____	6) $(4, -1), (14, 23)$ Distance = ____
	7) $(-3, 4), (-5, 0)$ Distance = ____	8) $(3, 9), (-1, 5)$ Distance = ____

Name:	Date: ....

Topic	**Finding Distance of Two Points - Answers**
Notes	✓ Use this formula to find the distance of two points A (x_1, y_1) and B (x_2, y_2): $$d = \sqrt{(x_2 - x_1)^2 + (y_2 - y_1)^2}$$
Example	***Find the distance of two points*** $(-1, 5)$ and $(4, -7)$. **Solution:** *Use distance of two points formula:* $d = \sqrt{(x_2 - x_1)^2 + (y_2 - y_1)^2}$ $(x_1, y_1) = (-1, 5)$, and $(x_2, y_2) = (4, -7)$ Then: $d = \sqrt{(x_2 - x_1)^2 + (y_2 - y_1)^2} \rightarrow d =$ $\sqrt{(4 - (-1))^2 + (-7 - 5)^2} = \sqrt{(-5)^2 + (-12)^2} = \sqrt{25 + 144} =$ $\sqrt{169} = 13$

Your Turn!	1) $(6, 2), (-4, 2)$ ***Distance*** $= 10$	2) $(2, -3), (2, 5)$ ***Distance*** $= 8$
	3) $(-5, 10), (7, 1)$ ***Distance*** $= 15$	4) $(8, 1), (-4, 6)$ ***Distance*** $= 13$
	5) $(-3, 6), (-4, 5)$ ***Distance*** $= \sqrt{2}$	6) $(4, -1), (14, 23)$ ***Distance*** $= 26$
	7) $(-3, 4), (-5, 0)$ ***Distance*** $= \sqrt{20} = 2\sqrt{5}$	8) $(3, 9), (-1, 5)$ ***Distance*** $= \sqrt{32} = 4\sqrt{2}$

Name:	Date: ....

Topic	**Multiplication Property of Exponents**
Notes	✓ Exponents are shorthand for repeated multiplication of the same number by itself. For example, instead of 2×2, we can write 2^2. For $3 \times 3 \times 3 \times 3$, we can write 3^4 ✓ In algebra, a variable is a letter used to stand for a number. The most common letters are: $x, y, z, a, b, c, m,$ and n. ✓ Exponent's rules: $x^a \times x^b = x^{a+b}$, $\frac{x^a}{x^b} = x^{a-b}$ $(x^a)^b = x^{a \times b}$ $\qquad$ $(xy)^a = x^a \times y^a$ $\qquad$ $(\frac{a}{b})^c = \frac{a^c}{b^c}$
Example	***Multiply.*** $4x^3 \times 2x^2$ Use Exponent's rules: $x^a \times x^b = x^{a+b} \rightarrow x^3 \times x^2 = x^{3+2} = x^5$ Then: $4x^3 \times 2x^2 = 8x^5$

Your Turn!	1) $x^2 \times 3x =$	2) $5x^4 \times x^2 =$
	3) $3x^2 \times 4x^5 =$	4) $3x^2 \times 6xy =$
	5) $3x^5y \times 5x^2y^3 =$	6) $3x^2y^2 \times 5x^2y^8 =$
	7) $5x^2y \times 5x^2y^7 =$	8) $6x^6 \times 4x^9y^4 =$
	9) $8x^2y^5 \times 7x^5y^3 =$	10) $12x^6x^2 \times 3xy^5 =$

Name:	Date: ....

Topic	**Multiplication Property of Exponents - Answers**
Notes	✓ Exponents are shorthand for repeated multiplication of the same number by itself. For example, instead of 2×2, we can write 2^2. For $3 \times 3 \times 3 \times 3$, we can write 3^4 ✓ In algebra, a variable is a letter used to stand for a number. The most common letters are: $x, y, z, a, b, c, m,$ and n. ✓ Exponent's rules: $x^a \times x^b = x^{a+b}$, $\frac{x^a}{x^b} = x^{a-b}$ $\qquad (x^a)^b = x^{a \times b} \qquad\qquad (xy)^a = x^a \times y^a \qquad\qquad \left(\frac{a}{b}\right)^c = \frac{a^c}{b^c}$
Example	*Multiply.* $4x^3 \times 2x^2$ Use Exponent's rules: $x^a \times x^b = x^{a+b} \rightarrow x^3 \times x^2 = x^{3+2} = x^5$ Then: $4x^3 \times 2x^2 = 8x^5$

Your Turn!	1) $x^2 \times 3x = 3x^3$	2) $5x^4 \times x^2 = 5x^6$
	3) $3x^2 \times 4x^5 = 12x^7$	4) $3x^2 \times 6xy = 18x^3y$
	5) $3x^5y \times 5x^2y^3 = 15x^7y^4$	6) $3x^2y^2 \times 5x^2y^8 = 15x^4y^{10}$
	7) $5x^2y \times 5x^2y^7 = 25x^4y^8$	8) $6x^6 \times 4x^9y^4 = 24x^{15}y^4$
	9) $8x^2y^5 \times 7x^5y^3 = 56x^7y^8$	10) $12x^6x^2 \times 3xy^5 = 36x^9y^5$

Name:	Date: ....

Topic	**Division Property of Exponents**
Notes	✓ For division of exponents use these formulas: $\frac{x^a}{x^b} = x^{a-b}$, $x \neq 0$ $\frac{x^a}{x^b} = \frac{1}{x^{b-a}}$, $x \neq 0$, $\frac{1}{x^b} = x^{-b}$
Example	*Simplify.* $\frac{6x^3 y}{36x^2 y^3}$ First cancel the common factor: $6 \rightarrow \frac{6x^3 y}{36x^2 y^3} = \frac{x^3 y}{6x^2 y^3}$ Use Exponent's rules: $\frac{x^a}{x^b} = x^{a-b} \rightarrow \frac{x^3}{x^2} = x^{3-2} = x^1 = x$ Then: $\frac{6x^3 y}{36x^2 y^3} = \frac{xy}{9y^3} \rightarrow$ now cancel the common factor: $y \rightarrow \frac{xy}{6y^3} = \frac{x}{6y^2}$

Your Turn!	1) $\frac{3^7}{3^2} =$	2) $\frac{5x}{10x^3} =$
	3) $\frac{3x^3}{2x^5} =$	4) $\frac{12x^3}{14x^6} =$
	5) $\frac{12x^3}{9y^8} =$	6) $\frac{25xy^4}{5x^6 y^2} =$
	7) $\frac{2x^4 y^5}{7xy^2} =$	8) $\frac{16x^2 y^8}{4x^3} =$
	9) $\frac{12x^4}{15x^7 y^9} =$	10) $\frac{12yx^4}{10yx^8} =$

Name: .... | **Date:** ....

Topic	Division Property of Exponents - Answers
Notes	✓ For division of exponents use following formulas: $\frac{x^a}{x^b} = x^{a-b}$, $x \neq 0$ $\frac{x^a}{x^b} = \frac{1}{x^{b-a}}$, $x \neq 0$, $\qquad \frac{1}{x^b} = x^{-b}$
Example	***Simplify.*** $\frac{6x^3y}{36x^2y^3}$ First cancel the common factor: $6 \rightarrow \frac{6x^3y}{36x^2y^3} = \frac{x^3y}{6x^2y^3}$ Use Exponent's rules: $\frac{x^a}{x^b} = x^{a-b} \rightarrow \frac{x^3}{x^2} = x^{3-2} = x^1 = x$ Then: $\frac{6x^3y}{36x^2y^3} = \frac{xy}{9y^3} \rightarrow$ now cancel the common factor: $y \rightarrow \frac{xy}{6y^3} = \frac{x}{6y^2}$

Your Turn!	1) $\frac{3^7}{3^2} = 3^5$	2) $\frac{5x}{10x^3} = \frac{1}{2x^2}$
	3) $\frac{3x^3}{2x^5} = \frac{3}{2x^2}$	4) $\frac{12x^3}{14x^6} = \frac{6}{7x^3}$
	5) $\frac{12x^3}{9y^8} = \frac{4x^3}{3y^8}$	6) $\frac{25xy^4}{5x^6y^2} = \frac{5y^2}{x^5}$
	7) $\frac{2x^4y^5}{7xy^2} = \frac{2x^3y^3}{7}$	8) $\frac{16x^2y^8}{4x^3} = \frac{4y^8}{x}$
	9) $\frac{12x^4}{15x^7y^9} = \frac{4}{5x^3y^9}$	10) $\frac{12y^8x^4}{10y^2x^8} = \frac{6y^6}{5x^4}$

Name:	Date: ....

Topic	**Powers of Products and Quotients**	
Notes	✓ For any nonzero numbers a and b and any integer x, $$(ab)^x = a^x \times b^x, \left(\frac{a}{b}\right)^c = \frac{a^c}{b^c}$$	
Example	**Simplify.** $\left(\frac{2x^3}{x}\right)^2$ First cancel the common factor: $x \to \left(\frac{2x^3}{x}\right)^2 = (2x^2)^2$ Use Exponent's rules: $(ab)^x = a^x \times b^x$ Then: $(2x^2)^2 = (2)^2(x^2)^2 = 4x^4$	
Your Turn!	1) $(4x^3x^3)^2 =$	2) $(3x^3 \times 5x)^2 =$
	3) $(10x^{11}y^3)^2 =$	4) $(9x^7y^5)^2 =$
	5) $(4x^4y^6)^3 =$	6) $(3x \times 4y^3)^2 =$
	7) $\left(\frac{5x}{x^2}\right)^2 =$	8) $\left(\frac{x^4y^4}{x^2y^2}\right)^3 =$
	9) $\left(\frac{25x}{5x^6}\right)^2 =$	10) $\left(\frac{x^8}{x^6y^2}\right)^2 =$

Name:	**Date:** ....

Topic	**Powers of Products and Quotients - Answers**
Notes	✓ For any nonzero numbers a and b and any integer x, $$(ab)^x = a^x \times b^x, \left(\frac{a}{b}\right)^c = \frac{a^c}{b^c}$$
Example	**Simplify**. $\left(\frac{2x^3}{x}\right)^2$ First cancel the common factor: $x \rightarrow \left(\frac{2x^3}{x}\right)^2 = \left(2x^2\right)^2$ Use Exponent's rules: $(ab)^x = a^x \times b^x$ Then: $\left(2x^2\right)^2 = (2)^2(x^2)^2 = 4x^4$
Your Turn!	1) $(4x^3 x^3)^2 = 16x^{12}$ 2) $(3x^3 \times 5x)^2 = 225x^8$ 3) $(10x^{11}y^3)^2 = 100x^{22}y^6$ 4) $(9x^7 y^5)^2 = 81x^{14}y^{10}$ 5) $(4x^4 y^6)^3 = 64\,x^{12}y^{18}$ 6) $(3x \times 4y^3)^2 = 144x^2 y^6$ 7) $\left(\frac{5x}{x^2}\right)^2 = \frac{25}{x^2}$ 8) $\left(\frac{x^4 y^4}{x^2 y^2}\right)^3 = x^6 y^6$ 9) $\left(\frac{25x}{5x^6}\right)^2 = \frac{25}{x^{10}}$ 10) $\left(\frac{x^8}{x^6 y^2}\right)^2 = \frac{x^4}{y^4}$

Name:	Date: ....

Topic	**Zero and Negative Exponents**
Notes	✓ A negative exponent is the reciprocal of that number with a positive exponent. $(3)^{-2} = \frac{1}{3^2}$ ✓ Zero-Exponent Rule: $a^0 = 1$, this means that anything raised to the zero power is 1. For example: $(28x^2y)^0 = 1$
Example	*Evaluate.* $\left(\frac{1}{3}\right)^{-2} =$ Use negative exponent's rule: $\left(\frac{1}{x^a}\right)^{-2} = (x^a)^2 \rightarrow \left(\frac{1}{3}\right)^{-2} = (3)^2 =$ Then: $(3)^2 = 9$

Your Turn!	1) $2^{-3} =$	2) $3^{-3} =$
	3) $7^{-3} =$	4) $1^{-3} =$
	5) $8^{-3} =$	6) $4^{-4} =$
	7) $10^{-3} =$	8) $7^{-4} =$
	9) $\left(\frac{1}{8}\right)^{-1} =$	10) $\left(\frac{1}{5}\right)^{-2} =$

Name:	Date: ....

Topic	**Zero and Negative Exponents - Answers**	
Notes	✓ A negative exponent is the reciprocal of that number with a positive exponent. $(3)^{-2} = \frac{1}{3^2}$ ✓ Zero-Exponent Rule: $a^0 = 1$, this means that anything raised to the zero power is 1. For example: $(28x^2 y)^0 = 1$	
Example	*Evaluate.* $\left(\frac{1}{3}\right)^{-2} =$ Use negative exponent's rule: $\left(\frac{1}{x^a}\right)^{-2} = (x^a)^2 \rightarrow \left(\frac{1}{3}\right)^{-2} = (3)^2 =$ Then: $(3)^2 = 9$	
Your Turn!	1) $2^{-3} = \frac{1}{8}$	2) $3^{-3} = \frac{1}{27}$
	3) $7^{-3} = \frac{1}{343}$	4) $1^{-3} = 1$
	5) $8^{-3} = \frac{1}{512}$	6) $4^{-4} = \frac{1}{256}$
	7) $10^{-3} = \frac{1}{1,000}$	8) $7^{-4} = \frac{1}{2,401}$
	9) $\left(\frac{1}{8}\right)^{-1} = 8$	10) $\left(\frac{1}{5}\right)^{-2} = 25$

Name:	Date: ....

Topic	**Negative Exponents and Negative Bases**
Notes	✓ Make the power positive. A negative exponent is the reciprocal of that number with a positive exponent. ✓ The parenthesis is important! 5^{-2} is not the same as $(-5)^{-2}$ $$(-5)^{-2} = -\frac{1}{5^2} \text{ and } (-5)^{-2} = +\frac{1}{5^2}$$
Example	*Simplify.* $\left(-\frac{3x}{4yz}\right)^{-2} =$ Use negative exponent's rule: $\left(\frac{x^a}{x^b}\right)^{-2} = \left(\frac{x^b}{x^a}\right)^2 \rightarrow \left(-\frac{3x}{4y}\right)^{-3} = \left(-\frac{4y}{3x}\right)^3$ Now use exponent's rule: $\left(\frac{a}{b}\right)^c = \frac{a^c}{b^c} \rightarrow \left(-\frac{4yz}{3x}\right)^3 = \frac{4^3y^3z^3}{3^3x^3} = \frac{64y^3z^3}{27x^3}$

Your Turn!	1) $-5x^{-2}y^{-3} =$	2) $20x^{-4}y^{-1} =$
	3) $14a^{-6}b^{-7} =$	4) $-12x^2y^{-3} =$
	5) $-\frac{25}{x^{-6}} =$	6) $\frac{7b}{-9c^{-4}} =$
	7) $\frac{7ab}{a^{-3}b^{-1}} =$	8) $-\frac{5n^{-2}}{10p^{-3}} = -$
	9) $\frac{4ab^{-2}}{-3c^{-2}} =$	10) $\left(\frac{3a}{2c}\right)^{-2} =$

Name:	Date: ....

Topic	**Negative Exponents and Negative Bases - Answers**	
Notes	✓ Make the power positive. A negative exponent is the reciprocal of that number with a positive exponent. ✓ The parenthesis is important! ✓ 5^{-2} is not the same as $(-5)^{-2}$ $\quad (-5)^{-2} = -\frac{1}{5^2}$ and $(-5)^{-2} = +\frac{1}{5^2}$	
Example	*Simplify.* $\left(-\frac{3x}{4yz}\right)^{-2} =$ Use negative exponent's rule: $\left(\frac{x^a}{x^b}\right)^{-2} = \left(\frac{x^b}{x^a}\right)^2 \rightarrow \left(-\frac{3x}{4yz}\right)^{-3} = \left(-\frac{4yz}{3x}\right)^3$ Now use exponent's rule: $\left(\frac{a}{b}\right)^c = \frac{a^c}{b^c} \rightarrow \left(-\frac{4yz}{3x}\right)^3 = \frac{4^3 y^3 z^3}{3^3 x^3} = \frac{64y^3 z^3}{27x^3}$	
Your Turn!	1) $-5x^{-2}y^{-3} = -\frac{5}{x^2 y^3}$	2) $20x^{-4}y^{-1} = \frac{20}{x^4 y}$
	3) $14a^{-6}b^{-7} = \frac{14}{a^6 b^7}$	4) $-12x^2 y^{-3} = -\frac{12x^2}{y^3}$
	5) $-\frac{25}{x^{-6}} = -25x^6$	6) $\frac{7b}{-9c^{-4}} = -\frac{7bc^4}{9}$
	7) $\frac{7ab}{a^{-3}b^{-1}} = 7a^4 b^2$	8) $-\frac{5n^{-2}}{10p^{-3}} = -\frac{p^3}{2n^2}$
	9) $\frac{4ab^{-2}}{-3c^{-2}} = -\frac{4ac^2}{3b^2}$	10) $\left(\frac{3a}{2c}\right)^{-2} = \frac{4c^2}{9a^2}$

| Name: .... | Date: .... |

Topic	Scientific Notation
Notes	✓ It is used to write very big or very small numbers in decimal form. ✓ In scientific notation all numbers are written in the form of: $$m \times 10^n$$ Decimal notation Scientific notation 3 3×10^0 $-45,000$ -4.5×10^4 0.3 3×10^{-1} 2,122.456 2.122456×10^3
Example	*Write 0.00054 in scientific notation.* First, move the decimal point to the right so that you have a number that is between 1 and 10. Then: $m = 5.4$ Now, determine how many places the decimal moved in step 1 by the power of 10. Then: 10^{-4} → When the decimal moved to the right, the exponent is negative. Then: $0.00054 = 5.4 \times 10^{-4}$
Your Turn!	1) $0.000325 =$ 2) $0.000023 =$ 3) $52,000,000 =$ 4) $21,000 =$ 5) $3 \times 10^{-1} =$ 6) $5 \times 10^{-2} =$ 7) $1.2 \times 10^3 =$ 8) $2 \times 10^{-4} =$

Name:	Date: ....

Topic	**Scientific Notation - Answers**	
Notes	✓ It is used to write very big or very small numbers in decimal form. ✓ In scientific notation all numbers are written in the form of: $$m \times 10^n$$ <table><tr><td>**Decimal notation**</td><td>**Scientific notation**</td></tr><tr><td>3</td><td>3×10^0</td></tr><tr><td>$-45,000$</td><td>-4.5×10^4</td></tr><tr><td>0.3</td><td>3×10^{-1}</td></tr><tr><td>2,122.456</td><td>2.122456×10^3</td></tr></table>	
Example	*Write 0.00054 in scientific notation.* First, move the decimal point to the right so that you have a number that is between 1 and 10. Then: $m = 5.4$ Now, determine how many places the decimal moved in step 1 by the power of 10. Then: $10^{-4} \rightarrow$ When the decimal moved to the right, the exponent is negative. Then: $0.00054 = 5.4 \times 10^{-4}$	
Your Turn!	1) $0.000325 = 3.25 \times 10^{-4}$	2) $0.00023 = 2.3 \times 10^{-5}$
	3) $52,000,000 = 5.2 \times 10^7$	4) $21,000 = 2.1 \times 10^4$
	5) $3 \times 10^{-1} = 0.3$	6) $5 \times 10^{-2} = 0.05$
	7) $1.2 \times 10^3 = 1,200$	8) $2 \times 10^{-4} = 0.0002$

Name:	Date: ....

Topic	Radicals
Notes	✓ If n is a positive integer and x is a real number, then: $\sqrt[n]{x} = x^{\frac{1}{n}}$, $\sqrt[n]{xy} = x^{\frac{1}{n}} \times y^{\frac{1}{n}}$, $\sqrt[n]{\frac{x}{y}} = \frac{x^{\frac{1}{n}}}{y^{\frac{1}{n}}}$, and $\sqrt[n]{x} \times \sqrt[n]{y} = \sqrt[n]{xy}$ ✓ A square root of x is a number r whose square is: $r^2 = x$ (r is a square root of x. ✓ To add and subtract radicals, we need to have the same values under the radical. For example: $\sqrt{3} + \sqrt{3} = 2\sqrt{3}$, $3\sqrt{5} - \sqrt{5} = 2\sqrt{5}$
Example	**Evaluate.** $\sqrt{32} + \sqrt{8} =$ **Solution:** Since we do not have the same values under the radical, we cannot add these two radicals. But we can simplify each radical. $\sqrt{32} = \sqrt{16} \times \sqrt{2} = 4\sqrt{2}$ and $\sqrt{8} = \sqrt{4} \times \sqrt{2} = 2\sqrt{2}$ Now, we have the same values under the radical. Then: $$\sqrt{32} + \sqrt{8} = 4\sqrt{2} + 2\sqrt{2} = 6\sqrt{2}$$
Your Turn!	1) $\sqrt{9} \times \sqrt{9} =$ 2) $\sqrt{8} \times \sqrt{2} =$ 3) $\sqrt{3} \times \sqrt{27} =$ 4) $\sqrt{32} \div \sqrt{2} =$ 5) $\sqrt{2} + \sqrt{8} =$ 6) $\sqrt{27} - \sqrt{3} =$ 7) $4\sqrt{5} - 2\sqrt{5} =$ 8) $3\sqrt{3} \times 2\sqrt{3} =$

Name:	Date: ....

Topic	Radicals - Answers
Notes	✓ If n is a positive integer and x is a real number, then: $\sqrt[n]{x} = x^{\frac{1}{n}}$, $\sqrt[n]{xy} = x^{\frac{1}{n}} \times y^{\frac{1}{n}}$, $\sqrt[n]{\frac{x}{y}} = \frac{x^{\frac{1}{n}}}{y^{\frac{1}{n}}}$, and $\sqrt[n]{x} \times \sqrt[n]{y} = \sqrt[n]{xy}$ ✓ A square root of x is a number r whose square is: $r^2 = x$ (r is a square root of x. ✓ To add and subtract radicals, we need to have the same values under the radical. For example: $\sqrt{3} + \sqrt{3} = 2\sqrt{3}$, $3\sqrt{5} - \sqrt{5} = 2\sqrt{5}$
Example	*Evaluate.* $\sqrt{32} + \sqrt{8} =$ **Solution:** Since we do not have the same values under the radical, we cannot add these two radicals. But we can simplify each radical. $\sqrt{32} = \sqrt{16} \times \sqrt{2} = 4\sqrt{2}$ and $\sqrt{8} = \sqrt{4} \times \sqrt{2} = 2\sqrt{2}$ Now, we have the same values under the radical. Then: $$\sqrt{32} + \sqrt{8} = 4\sqrt{2} + 2\sqrt{2} = 6\sqrt{2}$$

Your Turn!	1) $\sqrt{9} \times \sqrt{9} = 9$	2) $\sqrt{8} \times \sqrt{2} = 4$
	3) $\sqrt{3} \times \sqrt{27} = 9$	4) $\sqrt{32} \div \sqrt{2} = 4$
	5) $\sqrt{2} + \sqrt{8} = 3\sqrt{2}$	6) $\sqrt{27} - \sqrt{3} = 2\sqrt{3}$
	7) $4\sqrt{5} - 2\sqrt{5} = 2\sqrt{5}$	8) $3\sqrt{3} \times 2\sqrt{3} = 18$

Name:	Date: ....

Topic	**Simplifying Polynomials**
Notes	✓ Find "like" terms. (they have same variables with same power). ✓ Use "FOIL". (First–Out–In–Last) for binomials: $$(x + a)(x + b) = x^2 + (b + a)x + ab$$ ✓ Add or Subtract "like" terms using order of operation.
Example	***Simplify this expression.*** $(x + 3)(x - 8) =$ **Solution:** First apply FOIL method: $(a + b)(c + d) = ac + ad + bc + bd$ $(x + 3)(x - 8) = x^2 - 8x + 3x - 24$ Now combine like terms: $x^2 - 8x + 3x - 24 = x^2 - 5x - 24$

Your Turn!	1) $-(2x - 4) =$ _____	2) $2(2x + 6) =$ _____
	3) $3x(3x - 4) =$ _____	4) $5x(2x + 8) =$ _____
	5) $-2x(5x + 6) + 5x =$ _____	6) $-4x(8x - 3) - x^2 =$ _____
	7) $(x + 4)(x + 5) =$ _____	8) $(x + 2)(x + 8) =$ _____
	9) $-4x^2 + 10x^3 + 5x^2 =$ _____	10) $-3x^5 + 10x^4 + 5x^5 =$ _____

Name:	Date: ....

Topic	**Simplifying Polynomials - Answers**	
Notes	✓ Find "like" terms. (they have same variables with same power). ✓ Use "FOIL". (First–Out–In–Last) for binomials: $$(x + a)(x + b) = x^2 + (b + a)x + ab$$ ✓ Add or Subtract "like" terms using order of operation.	
Example	***Simplify this expression***. $(x + 3)(x - 8) =$ **Solution:** First apply FOIL method: $(a + b)(c + d) = ac + ad + bc + bd$ $(x + 3)(x - 8) = x^2 - 8x + 3x - 24$ Now combine like terms: $x^2 - 8x + 3x - 24 = x^2 - 5x - 24$	
Your Turn!	1) $-(2x - 4) =$ $-2x + 4$	2) $2(2x + 6) =$ $4x + 12$
	3) $3x(3x - 4) =$ $9x^2 - 12x$	4) $5x(2x + 8) =$ $10x^2 + 40x$
	5) $-2x(5x + 6) + 5x =$ $-10x^2 - 7x$	6) $-4x(8x - 3) - x^2 =$ $-33x^2 + 12x$
	7) $(x + 4)(x + 5) =$ $x^2 + 9x + 20$	8) $(x + 2)(x + 8) =$ $x^2 + 10x + 16$
	9) $-4x^2 + 10x^3 + 5x^2 =$ $10x^3 + x^2$	10) $-3x^5 + 10x^4 + 5x^5 =$ $2x^5 + 10x^4$

| Name: .... | Date: .... |

Topic	**Adding and Subtracting Polynomials**
Notes	✓ Adding polynomials is just a matter of combining like terms, with some order of operations considerations thrown in. ✓ Be careful with the minus signs, and don't confuse addition and multiplication!
Example	***Simplify the expressions.*** $(3x^2 - 4x^3) - (5x^3 - 8x^2) =$ **Solution:** First use Distributive Property: $-(5x^3 - 8x^2) = -5x^3 + 8x^2$ $\rightarrow (3x^2 - 4x^3) - (5x^3 - 8x^2) = 3x^2 - 4x^3 - 5x^3 + 8x^2$ Now combine like terms: $3x^2 - 4x^3 - 5x^3 + 8x^2 = -9x^3 + 11x^2$

Your Turn!

1) $(x^2 - x) + (4x^2 - 5) =$
_____

2) $(2x^3 + x) - (x^3 + 2) =$
_____

3) $(x^2 - 5x) + (6x^2 - 5) =$
_____

4) $(8x^2 - 2) - (3x^2 + 7) =$
_____

5) $(3x^2 + 2) - (2 - 4x^2) =$
_____

6) $(x^3 + x^2) - (x^3 - 10) =$
_____

7) $(3x^3 - 2x) - (x - x^3) =$
_____

8) $(x - 5x^4) - (2x^4 + 3x) =$
_____

9) $(6x^3 + 5) - (4 - 5x^3) =$
_____

10) $(2x^2 + 5x^3) - (6x^3 + 7) =$
_____

Name:	Date: ....

Topic	**Adding and Subtracting Polynomials - Answers**	
Notes	✓ Adding polynomials is just a matter of combining like terms, with some order of operations considerations thrown in. ✓ Be careful with the minus signs, and don't confuse addition and multiplication!	
Example	*Simplify the expressions.* $(3x^2 - 4x^3) - (5x^3 - 8x^2) =$ **Solution:** First use Distributive Property: $-(5x^3 - 8x^2) = -5x^3 + 8x^2$ $\rightarrow (3x^2 - 4x^3) - (5x^3 - 8x^2) = 3x^2 - 4x^3 - 5x^3 + 8x^2$ Now combine like terms: $3x^2 - 4x^3 - 5x^3 + 8x^2 = -9x^3 + 11x^2$	

Your Turn!	1) $(x^2 - x) + (4x^2 - 5) =$ $5x^2 - x - 5$	2) $(2x^3 + x) - (x^3 + 2) =$ $x^3 + x - 2$
	3) $(x^2 - 5x) + (6x^2 - 5) =$ $7x^2 - 5x - 5$	4) $(8x^2 - 2) - (3x^2 + 7) =$ $5x^2 - 9$
	5) $(3x^2 + 2) - (2 - 4x^2) =$ $7x^2$	6) $(x^3 + x^2) - (x^3 - 10) =$ $x^2 + 10$
	7) $(3x^3 - 2x) - (x - x^3) =$ $4x^3 - 3x$	8) $(x - 5x^4) - (2x^4 + 3x) =$ $7x^4 - 2x$
	9) $(6x^3 + 5) - (4 - 5x^3) =$ $11x^3 + 1$	10) $(2x^2 + 5x^3) - (6x^3 + 7) =$ $-x^3 + 2x^2 - 7$

Name: …………………………………….	Date: ………………………………………

Topic	**Multiplying Binomials**	
Notes	✓ A binomial is a polynomial that is the sum or the difference of two terms, each of which is a monomial. ✓ To multiply two binomials, use "FOIL" method. (First–Out–In–Last) $(x + a)(x + b) = x \times x + x \times b + a \times x + a \times b = x^2 + bx + ax + ab$	
Example	**Multiply.** $(x - 4)(x + 9) =$ **Solution:** Use "FOIL". (First–Out–In–Last): $(x - 4)(x + 9) = x^2 + 9x - 4x - 36$ Then simplify: $x^2 + 9x - 4x - 36 = x^2 + 5x - 36$	
Your Turn!	1) $(x + 2)(x + 2) =$ _____	2) $(x + 3)(x + 2) =$ _____
	3) $(x - 3)(x + 4) =$ _____	4) $(x - 2)(x - 4) =$ _____
	5) $(x + 3)(x + 4) =$ _____	6) $(x + 5)(x + 4) =$ _____
	7) $(x - 6)(x - 5) =$ _____	8) $(x - 5)(x - 5) =$ _____
	9) $(x + 6)(x - 8) =$ _____	10) $(x - 9)(x + 7) =$ _____

Name:	Date: ....

Topic	**Multiplying Binomials - Answers**	
Notes	✓ A binomial is a polynomial that is the sum or the difference of two terms, each of which is a monomial. ✓ To multiply two binomials, use "FOIL" method. (First–Out–In–Last) $(x + a)(x + b) = x \times x + x \times b + a \times x + a \times b = x^2 + bx + ax + ab$	
Example	***Multiply.*** $(x - 4)(x + 9) =$ **Solution:** Use "FOIL". (First–Out–In–Last): $(x - 4)(x + 9) = x^2 + 9x - 4x - 36$ Then simplify: $x^2 + 9x - 4x - 36 = x^2 + 5x - 36$	
Your Turn!	1) $(x + 2)(x + 2) =$ $x^2 + 4x + 4$	2) $(x + 3)(x + 2) =$ $x^2 + 5x + 6$
	3) $(x - 3)(x + 4) =$ $x^2 + x - 12$	4) $(x - 2)(x - 4) =$ $x^2 - 6x + 8$
	5) $(x + 3)(x + 4) =$ $x^2 + 7x + 12$	6) $(x + 5)(x + 4) =$ $x^2 + 9x + 20$
	7) $(x - 6)(x - 5) =$ $x^2 - 11x + 30$	8) $(x - 5)(x - 5) =$ $x^2 - 10x + 25$
	9) $(x + 6)(x - 8) =$ $x^2 - 2x - 48$	10) $(x - 9)(x + 7) =$ $x^2 - 2x - 63$

Name:	Date: ....

Topic	**Multiplying and Dividing Monomials**	
Notes	✓ When you divide or multiply two monomials you need to divide or multiply their coefficients and then divide or multiply their variables. ✓ In case of exponents with the same base, you need to subtract their powers. ✓ Exponent's rules: $$x^a \times x^b = x^{a+b}, \qquad \frac{x^a}{x^b} = x^{a-b}$$ $$\frac{1}{x^b} = x^{-b}, \quad (x^a)^b = x^{a \times b}$$ $$(xy)^a = x^a \times y^a$$	
Example	*Divide expressions.* $\frac{-18x^5y^6}{2xy^2} =$ **Solution:** Use exponents' division rule: $\frac{x^a}{x^b} = x^{a-b}, \frac{x^5}{x} = x^{5-1} = x^4$ and $\frac{y^6}{y^2} = y^4$ Then: $\frac{-18x^5y^6}{2xy^2} = -9x^4y^4$	
Your Turn!	1) $(x^8y)(xy^2) =$ _____	2) $(x^4y^3)(x^2y^3) =$ _____
	3) $(x^7y^4)(2x^5y^2) =$ _____	4) $(3x^5y^4)(4x^6y^3) =$ _____
	5) $(-6x^8y^7)(4x^6y^9) =$ _____	6) $(-2x^9y^3)(9x^7y^8) =$ _____
	7) $\frac{30x^8y^9}{6x^5y^4} =$ _____	8) $\frac{-42x^{12}y^{16}}{7x^8y^9} =$ _____

Name:	Date: ....

Topic	**Multiplying and Dividing Monomials - Answers**	
Notes	✓ When you divide or multiply two monomials you need to divide or multiply their coefficients and then divide or multiply their variables. ✓ In case of exponents with the same base, you need to subtract their powers. ✓ Exponent's rules: $$x^a \times x^b = x^{a+b}, \qquad \frac{x^a}{x^b} = x^{a-b}$$ $$\frac{1}{x^b} = x^{-b}, \quad (x^a)^b = x^{a \times b}$$ $$(xy)^a = x^a \times y^a$$	
Example	*Divide expressions*. $\dfrac{-18x^5y^6}{2xy^2} =$ **Solution:** Use exponents' division rule: $\dfrac{x^a}{x^b} = x^{a-b}$, $\dfrac{x^5}{x} = x^{5-1} = x^4$ and $\dfrac{y^6}{y^2} = y^4$ Then: $\dfrac{-18x^5y^6}{2xy^2} = -9x^4y^4$	
Your Turn!	1) $(x^8y)(xy^2) =$ x^9y^3	2) $(x^4y^3)(x^2y^3) =$ x^6y^6
	3) $(x^7y^4)(2x^5y^2) =$ $2x^{12}y^6$	4) $(3x^5y^4)(4x^6y^3) =$ $12x^{11}y^7$
	5) $(-6x^8y^7)(4x^6y^9) =$ $-24x^{14}y^{16}$	6) $(-2x^9y^3)(9x^7y^8) =$ $-18x^{16}y^{11}$
	7) $\dfrac{30x^8y^9}{6x^5y^4} =$ $5x^3y^5$	8) $\dfrac{-42x^{12}y^{16}}{7x^8y^9} =$ $-6x^4y^7$

Name:	Date: ....

Topic	Multiplying a Polynomial and a Monomial
Notes	✓ When multiplying monomials, use the product rule for exponents. $x^a \times x^b = x^{a+b}$ ✓ When multiplying a monomial by a polynomial, use the distributive property. $$a \times (b + c) = a \times b + a \times c = ab + ac$$ $$a \times (b - c) = a \times b - a \times c = ab - ac$$
Example	*Multiply expressions.* $4x(5x - 8) =$ **Solution:** Use Distributive Property: $4x(5x - 8) = 4x \times 5x - 4x \times (8) =$ Now, simplify: $4x \times 5x - 4x \times (8) = 20x^2 - 32x$
Your Turn!	1) $3x(2x + y) =$ ____ 2) $x(x - 3y) =$ ____ 3) $-x(5x - 3y) =$ ____ 4) $4x(x + 5y) =$ ____ 5) $-x(5x + 8y) =$ ____ 6) $2x(6x - 7y) =$ ____ 7) $-3x(x^3 + 4y^2 - 6x) =$ ____ 8) $7x(x^2 - 5y^2 + 4) =$ ____

Name: ……………………………….	Date: ……………………………………

Topic	**Multiplying a Polynomial and a Monomial - Answers**	
Notes	✓ When multiplying monomials, use the product rule for exponents. $x^a \times x^b = x^{a+b}$ ✓ When multiplying a monomial by a polynomial, use the distributive property. $$a \times (b + c) = a \times b + a \times c = ab + ac$$ $$a \times (b - c) = a \times b - a \times c = ab - ac$$	
Example	***Multiply expressions.*** $4x(5x - 8) =$ **Solution:** Use Distributive Property: $4x(5x - 8) = 4x \times 5x - 4x \times (8) =$ Now, simplify: $4x \times 5x - 4x \times (8) = 20x^2 - 32x$	
Your Turn!	1) $3x(2x + y) =$ $6x^2 + 3xy$	2) $x(x - 3y) =$ $x^2 - 3xy$
	3) $-x(5x - 3y) =$ $-5x^2 + 3xy$	4) $4x(x + 5y) =$ $4x^2 + 20xy$
	5) $-x(5x + 8y) =$ $-5x^2 - 8xy$	6) $2x(6x - 7y) =$ $12x^2 - 14xy$
	7) $-3x(x^3 + 4y^2 - 6x) =$ $-3x^4 - 12xy^2 + 18x^2$	8) $7x(x^2 - 5y^2 + 4) =$ $7x^3 - 35xy^2 + 28x$

Name:	Date: ....

Topic	Multiplying Monomials	
Notes	✓ A monomial is a polynomial with just one term: Examples: $5x$ or $7x^2yz^8$. ✓ When you multiply monomials, first multiply the coefficients (a number placed before and multiplying the variable) and then multiply the variables using multiplication property of exponents. $x^a \times x^b = x^{a+b}$	
Example	*Multiply.* $(-3xy^4z^5) \times (2x^2y^5z^3) =$ **Solution:** Multiply coefficients and find same variables and use multiplication property of exponents: $x^a \times x^b = x^{a+b}$ $-3 \times 2 = -6$, $x \times x^2 = x^{1+2} = x^3$, $y^4 \times y^5 = y^{4+5} = y^9$, and $z^2 \times z^5 = z^{2+5} = z^7$ Then: $(-3xy^4z^5) \times (2x^2y^5z^3) = -6x^3y^9z^7$	
Your Turn!	1) $2x^2 \times 4x^6 =$ _____	2) $5x^7 \times 6x^4 =$ _____
	3) $-2x^2y^4 \times 6x^3y^2 =$ _____	4) $-5x^5y \times 3x^3y^4 =$ _____
	5) $8x^7y^5 \times 5x^6y^3 =$ _____	6) $-6x^7y^5 \times (-3x^9y^8) =$ _____
	7) $12x^8y^8z^4 \times 3x^4y^3z =$ _____	8) $-8x^9y^7z^{11} \times 7x^6y^7z^5 =$ _____

Name:	Date: ....

Topic	Multiplying Monomials
Notes	✓ A monomial is a polynomial with just one term: Examples: $5x$ or $7x^2yz^8$. ✓ When you multiply monomials, first multiply the coefficients (a number placed before and multiplying the variable) and then multiply the variables using multiplication property of exponents. $x^a \times x^b = x^{a+b}$
Example	*Multiply*. $(-3xy^4z^5) \times (2x^2y^5z^3) =$ **Solution:** Multiply coefficients and find same variables and use multiplication property of exponents: $x^a \times x^b = x^{a+b}$ $-3 \times 2 = -6$, $x \times x^2 = x^{1+2} = x^3$, $y^4 \times y^5 = y^{4+5} = y^9$, and $z^2 \times z^5 = z^{2+5} = z^7$ Then: $(-3xy^4z^5) \times (2x^2y^5z^3) = -6x^3y^9z^7$

Your Turn!	1) $2x^2 \times 4x^6 =$ $8x^8$	2) $5x^7 \times 6x^4 =$ $30x^{11}$
	3) $-2x^2y^4 \times 6x^3y^2 =$ $-12x^5y^6$	4) $-5x^5y \times 3x^3y^4 =$ $-15x^8y^5$
	5) $8x^7y^5 \times 5x^6y^3 =$ $40x^{13}y^8$	6) $-6x^7y^5 \times (-3x^9y^8) =$ $18x^{16}y^{13}$
	7) $12x^8y^8z^4 \times 3x^4y^3z =$ $36x^{12}y^{11}z^5$	8) $-8x^9y^7z^{11} \times 7x^6y^7z^5 =$ $-56x^{15}y^{14}z^{16}$

Name:	Date: ....

Topic	Factoring Trinomials
Notes	To factor trinomial, use of the following methods: ✓ "FOIL": $(x + a)(x + b) = x^2 + (b + a)x + ab$ ✓ "Difference of Squares": $$a^2 - b^2 = (a + b)(a - b)$$ $$a^2 + 2ab + b^2 = (a + b)(a + b)$$ $$a^2 - 2ab + b^2 = (a - b)(a - b)$$ ✓ "Reverse FOIL": $x^2 + (b + a)x + ab = (x + a)(x + b)$
Example	***Factor this trinomial.*** $x^2 + 12x + 32 =$ **Solution:** Break the expression into groups: $(x^2 + 4x) + (8x + 32)$ Now factor out x from $x^2 + 4x : x(x + 4)$, and factor out 8 from $8x + 32$: $8(x + 4)$ Then: $(x^2 + 4x) + (8x + 32) = x(x + 4) + 8(x + 4)$ Now factor out like term: $(x + 4) \rightarrow (x + 4)(x + 8)$

Your Turn!	1) $x^2 + 6x + 9 =$ _____	2) $x^2 + 5x + 6 =$ _____
	3) $x^2 + x + 12 =$ _____	4) $x^2 - 6x + 8 =$ _____
	5) $x^2 + 7x + 12 =$ _____	6) $x^2 + 12x + 32 =$ _____
	7) $x^2 - 11x + 30 =$ _____	8) $x^2 - 14x + 45 =$ _____

Name:	Date: ....

Topic	**Factoring Trinomials - Answers**
Notes	To factor trinomial, use of the following methods: ✓ "FOIL": $(x + a)(x + b) = x^2 + (b + a)x + ab$ ✓ "Difference of Squares": $$a^2 - b^2 = (a + b)(a - b)$$ $$a^2 + 2ab + b^2 = (a + b)(a + b)$$ $$a^2 - 2ab + b^2 = (a - b)(a - b)$$ ✓ "Reverse FOIL": $x^2 + (b + a)x + ab = (x + a)(x + b)$
Example	**Factor this trinomial.** $x^2 + 12x + 32 =$ **Solution:** Break the expression into groups: $(x^2 + 4x) + (8x + 32)$ Now factor out x from $x^2 + 4x$: $x(x + 4)$, and factor out 8 from $8x + 32$: $8(x + 4)$ Then: $(x^2 + 4x) + (8x + 32) = x(x + 4) + 8(x + 4)$ Now factor out like term: $(x + 4) \rightarrow (x + 4)(x + 8)$

Your Turn!	1) $x^2 + 6x + 9 =$ $(x + 3)(x + 3)$	2) $x^2 + 5x + 6 =$ $(x + 3)(x + 2)$
	3) $x^2 + x + 12 =$ $(x - 3)(x + 4)$	4) $x^2 - 6x + 8 =$ $(x - 2)(x - 4)$
	5) $x^2 + 7x + 12 =$ $(x + 3)(x + 4)$	6) $x^2 + 12x + 32 =$ $(x + 8)(x + 4)$
	7) $x^2 - 11x + 30 =$ $(x - 6)(x - 5)$	8) $x^2 - 14x + 45 =$ $(x - 9)(x - 5)$

| Name: .... | Date: .... |

Topic	**The Pythagorean Theorem**
Notes	✓ In any right triangle: $a^2 + b^2 = c^2$
Example	Right triangle ABC (not shown) has two legs of lengths 18 cm (AB) and 24 cm (AC). What is the length of the third side (BC)? **Solution:** Use Pythagorean Theorem: $a^2 + b^2 = c^2$ Then: $a^2 + b^2 = c^2 \rightarrow 18^2 + 24^2 = c^2 \rightarrow 324 + 576 = c^2$ $c^2 = 900 \rightarrow c = \sqrt{900} = 30\ cm$
Your Turn!	1) _____ 15, ?, 8 2) _____ 34, 16, ? 3) _____ 13, 5, ? 4) _____ 15, ?, 12

Name:	Date: ....

Topic	**The Pythagorean Theorem - Answers**
Notes	✓ In any right triangle: $a^2 + b^2 = c^2$
Example	Right triangle ABC (not shown) has two legs of lengths 18 cm (AB) and 24 cm (AC). What is the length of the third side (BC)? **Solution:** Use Pythagorean Theorem: $a^2 + b^2 = c^2$ Then: $a^2 + b^2 = c^2 \rightarrow 18^2 + 24^2 = c^2 \rightarrow 324 + 576 = c^2$ $c^2 = 900 \rightarrow c = \sqrt{900} = 30 \ cm$
Your Turn!	1) 17 ... 2) 30 ... 3) 12 ... 4) 9

1) 17

15, ?, 8

2) 30

34, 16, ?

3) 12

13, 5, ?

4) 9

15, ?, 12

Name: …………………………………….		Date: ……………………………………

Topic	Triangles	
Notes	✓ In any triangle the sum of all angles is 180 degrees. ✓ Area of a triangle = $\frac{1}{2}$ $(base \times height)$	
Example	**What is the area of the following triangle?** **Solution:** Use the area formula: Area = $\frac{1}{2}$ $(base \times height)$ $base = 16$ and $height = 6$ Area = $\frac{1}{2}(16 \times 6) = \frac{96}{2} = 48$	
Your Turn!	5) _____ 24 10 7) _____ 20 30	6) _____ 18 28 8) _____ 32 46

| Name: .... | Date: .... |

Topic	**Triangles - Answers**
Notes	✓ In any triangle the sum of all angles is 180 degrees. ✓ Area of a triangle = $\frac{1}{2}$ $(base \times height)$ h b
Example	**What is the area of the following triangle?** 6 16 **Solution:** Use the area formula: Area = $\frac{1}{2}$ $(base \times height)$ $base = 16$ and $height = 6$ Area = $\frac{1}{2}(16 \times 6) = \frac{96}{2} = 48$
Your Turn!	5) 120 24 10 6) 252 18 28 7) 300 20 30 8) 736 32 46

| Name: .... | Date: .... |

Topic	Polygons
Notes	Perimeter of a square $= 4 \times side = 4s$ Perimeter of a rectangle $= 2(width + length)$ Perimeter of trapezoid $= a + b + c + d$ Perimeter of a regular hexagon $= 6a$ Perimeter of a parallelogram $= 2(l + w)$

| **Example** | **Find the perimeter of following regular hexagon.**

Solution: Since the hexagon is regular, all sides are equal. Then: Perimeter of Hexagon $= 6 \times (one\ side)$
Perimeter of Hexagon $= 6 \times (one\ side) = 6 \times 9 = 54\ m$ |

Your Turn!

9) *(rectangle)* _____

15 *in*, 9 *in*

10) _____

8 m, 10 m, 10 m, 14 m

11) *(regular hexagon)* 5 *m* _____

12) *(parallelogram)*_____

16 *in*, 10 *in*

Name: ....

Date: ....

Topic	Polygons - Answers
Notes	Perimeter of a square $= 4 \times side = 4s$ Perimeter of a rectangle $= 2(width + length)$ Perimeter of trapezoid $= a + b + c + d$ Perimeter of a regular hexagon $= 6a$ Perimeter of a parallelogram $= 2(l + w)$

Example

Find the perimeter of following regular hexagon.

Solution: Since the hexagon is regular, all sides are equal. Then: Perimeter of Hexagon $= 6 \times (one\ side)$
Perimeter of Hexagon $= 6 \times (one\ side) = 6 \times 9 = 54\ m$

Your Turn!

9) *(rectangle)* 48 in

9 in
15 in

10) 42 m

8 m
10 m   10 m
14 m

11) *(regular hexagon)* 30 m

5 m

12) *(parallelogram)* 52 in

10 in
16 in

Name:	Date: ....

Topic	**Circles**
Notes	✓ In a circle, variable r is usually used for the radius and d for diameter and π is about 3.14. ✓ $Area\ of\ a\ circle = \pi r^2$ ✓ $Circumference\ of\ a\ circle = 2\pi r$ r
Example	*Find the area of the circle.* **Solution:** Use area formula: $Area = \pi r^2$ $r = 2\ in \rightarrow Area = \pi(2)^2 = 4\pi, \pi = 3.14$ **Then:** $Area = 4 \times 3.14 = 12.56\ in^2$ $2\ in$
Your Turn!	***Find the area of each circle.*** ($\pi = 3.14$) 1) _____ $6\ cm$ 2) _____ $10\ in$ ***Find the Circumference of each circle.*** ($\pi = 3.14$) 3) _____ $8\ cm$ 4) _____ $6\ m$

Name:	Date: ....

Topic	**Circles - Answers**	
Notes	✓ In a circle, variable r is usually used for the radius and d for diameter and π is about 3.14. ✓ $Area\ of\ a\ circle = \pi r^2$ ✓ $Circumference\ of\ a\ circle = 2\pi r$	r
Example	**Find the area of the circle.** **Solution:** Use area formula: $Area = \pi r^2$ $r = 2\ in \rightarrow Area = \pi(2)^2 = 4\pi, \pi = 3.14$ **Then:** $Area = 4 \times 3.14 = 12.56\ in^2$	$2\ in$
Your Turn!	**Find the area of each circle.** ($\pi = 3.14$) 1) $113.04\ cm^2$ 6 cm 2) $314\ in^2$ 10 in **Find the Circumference of each circle.** ($\pi = 3.14$) 3) $50.24\ cm$ 8 cm 4) $37.68\ m$ 6 m	

Name:	**Date:** ....

Topic	Cubes
Notes	✓ A cube is a three-dimensional solid object bounded by six square sides. ✓ Volume is the measure of the amount of space inside of a solid figure, like a cube, ball, cylinder or pyramid. ✓ Volume of a cube $= (one\ side)^3$ ✓ surface area of cube $= 6 \times (one\ side)^2$
Example	***Find the volume and surface area of the following cube.*** 15 cm **Solution:** Use volume formula: $volume = (one\ side)^3$ Then: $volume = (one\ side)^3 = (15)^3 = 3,375\ cm^3$ Use surface area formula: $surface\ area\ of\ cube: 6(one\ side)^2 = 6(15)^2 = 6(225) = 1,350\ cm^2$
Your Turn!	***Find the volume of each cube.*** 1) _____ 11 in 2) _____ 13 ft 3) _____ 14 cm 4) _____ 30 m

Name: ....

Date: ....

Topic	Cubes - Answers
Notes	✓ A cube is a three-dimensional solid object bounded by six square sides. ✓ Volume is the measure of the amount of space inside of a solid figure, like a cube, ball, cylinder or pyramid. ✓ Volume of a cube $= (one\ side)^3$ ✓ surface area of cube $= 6 \times (one\ side)^2$
Example	**Find the volume and surface area of the following cube.** 15 cm **Solution:** Use volume formula: $volume = (one\ side)^3$ Then: $volume = (one\ side)^3 = (15)^3 = 3{,}375\ cm^3$ Use surface area formula: $surface\ area\ of\ cube: 6(one\ side)^2 = 6(15)^2 = 6(225) = 1{,}350\ cm^2$
Your Turn!	**Find the volume of each cube.** 1) $1{,}331\ in^3$ 11 in 2) $2{,}197\ ft^3$ 13 ft 3) $2{,}744\ cm^3$ 14 cm 4) $27{,}000\ m^3$ 30 m

Name: …………………………………..	Date: ………………………………………

Topic	Trapezoids
Notes	✓ A quadrilateral with at least one pair of parallel sides is a trapezoid. ✓ Area of a trapezoid $= \frac{1}{2}h(b_1 + b_2)$ b_2 h b_1
Example	***Calculate the area of the trapezoid.*** **Solution:** Use area formula: $A = \frac{1}{2}h(b_1 + b_2)$ $b_1 = 8\ cm$, $b_2 = 12\ cm$ and $h = 14\ cm$ Then: $A = \frac{1}{2}(14)(12 + 8) = 7(20) = 140\ cm^2$ $12\ cm$ $14\ cm$ $8\ cm$
Your Turn!	1) _____ 5 cm 4 cm 9 cm 2) _____ 8 m 10 m 12 m 3) _____ 7 ft 6 ft 15 ft 4) _____ 10 cm 8 cm 14 cm

Name:	Date: ....

Topic	**Trapezoids - Answers**	
Notes	✓ A quadrilateral with at least one pair of parallel sides is a trapezoid. ✓ Area of a trapezoid $= \frac{1}{2}h(b_1 + b_2)$	

Example	**Calculate the area of the trapezoid.**
	   Solution:
	   Use area formula: $A = \frac{1}{2}h(b_1 + b_2)$
	 $b_1 = 8\ cm$, $b_2 = 12\ cm$ and $h = 14\ cm$
	 Then: $A = \frac{1}{2}(14)(12 + 8) = 7(20) = 140\ cm^2$	

Your Turn!	1) $28\ cm^2$ 2) $100\ m^2$ 3) $66\ ft^2$ 4) $96\ cm^2$	

Name:	Date: ....

Topic	**Rectangular Prisms**
Notes	✓ A solid 3-dimensional object which has six rectangular faces. ✓ Volume of a Rectangular prism $= \boldsymbol{Length \times Width \times Height}$ $Volume = l \times w \times h$ $Surface\ area = 2(wh + lw + lh)$
Example	***Find the volume and surface area of rectangular prism.*** **Solution:** Use volume formula: $Volume = l \times w \times h$ Then: $Volume = 4 \times 2 \times 6 = 48\ m^3$ Use surface area formula: $Surface\ area = 2(wh + lw + lh)$ Then: $Surface\ area = 2\big((2 \times 6) + (4 \times 2) + (4 \times 6)\big)$ $\qquad\qquad = 2(12 + 8 + 24) = 2(44) = 88\ m^2$
Your Turn!	***Find the surface area of each Rectangular Prism.*** 1) _____ 6 ft 10 ft 4 ft 2) _____ 8 cm 16 cm 6 cm 3) _____ 12 m 18 m 10 m 4) _____ 20 in 15 in 12 in

Name: ....

Date: ....

Topic	**Rectangular Prisms - Answers**
Notes	✓ A solid 3-dimensional object which has six rectangular faces. ✓ Volume of a Rectangular prism = **Length × Width × Height** $Volume = l \times w \times h$ $Surface\ area = 2(wh + lw + lh)$
Example	***Find the volume and surface area of rectangular prism.*** **Solution:** Use volume formula: $Volume = l \times w \times h$ Then: $Volume = 4 \times 2 \times 6 = 48\ m^3$ Use surface area formula: $Surface\ area = 2(wh + lw + lh)$ Then: $Surface\ area = 2\big((2 \times 6) + (4 \times 2) + (4 \times 6)\big)$ $= 2(12 + 8 + 24) = 2(44) = 88\ m^2$
Your Turn!	***Find the surface area of each Rectangular Prism.*** 1) $248\ ft^2$ 6 ft, 10 ft, 4 ft 2) $544\ cm^2$ 8 cm, 16 cm, 6 cm 3) $1,032\ m^2$ 12 m, 18 m, 10 m 4) $1,440\ in^2$ 20 in, 15 in, 12 in

Name:	Date: ....

Topic	**Cylinder**
Notes	✓ A cylinder is a solid geometric figure with straight parallel sides and a circular or oval cross section. ✓ $Volume\ of\ Cylinder\ Formula = \pi(radius)^2 \times height\ \ \pi = 3.14$ ✓ $Surface\ area\ of\ a\ cylinder = 2\pi r^2 + 2\pi rh$

Example

Find the volume and Surface area of the follow Cylinder.

Solution:
Use volume formula: $Volume = \pi(radius)^2 \times height$
Then: $Volume = \pi(3)^2 \times 12 = 9\pi \times 12 = 108\pi$
$\pi = 3.14$ ***then:*** $Volume = 108\pi = 339.12\ cm^3$
Use surface area formula: $Surface\ area = 2\pi r^2 + 2\pi rh$
Then: $2\pi(3)^2 + 2\pi(3)(12) = 2\pi(9) + 2\pi(36) = 18\pi + 72\pi = 90\pi$
$\pi = 3.14$ ***Then:*** $Surface\ area = 90 \times 3.14 = 282.6\ cm^2$

Your Turn!

Find the volume of each Cylinder. $(\pi = 3.14)$

1) _____
10 in
2 in

2) _____
14 m
5 m

Find the Surface area of each Cylinder. $(\pi = 3.14)$

3) _____
15 ft
9 ft

4) _____
20 cm
12 cm

Name:	Date: ....

Topic	Cylinder - Answers

| **Notes** | ✓ A cylinder is a solid geometric figure with straight parallel sides and a circular or oval cross section.
✓ *Volume of Cylinder Formula* $= \pi(radius)^2 \times height$ $\pi = 3.14$
✓ *Surface area of a cylinder* $= 2\pi r^2 + 2\pi rh$ |

| **Example** | **Find the volume and Surface area of the follow Cylinder.**

Solution:
Use volume formula: $Volume = \pi(radius)^2 \times height$
Then: $Volume = \pi(3)^2 \times 12 = 9\pi \times 12 = 108\pi$
$\pi = 3.14$ *then:* $Volume = 108\pi = 339.12\ cm^3$
Use surface area formula: $Surface\ area = 2\pi r^2 + 2\pi rh$
Then: $2\pi(3)^2 + 2\pi(3)(12) = 2\pi(9) + 2\pi(36) = 18\pi + 72\pi = 90\pi$
$\pi = 3.14$ **Then:** $Surface\ area = 90 \times 3.14 = 282.6\ cm^2$ |

| **Your Turn!** | **Find the volume of each Cylinder.** ($\pi = 3.14$)

1) $125.6\ in^3$ 2) $1{,}099\ m^3$
10 in, 2 in   14 m, 5 m

Find the Surface area of each Cylinder. ($\pi = 3.14$)

3) $1{,}356.48\ ft^2$ 4) $2{,}411.52\ cm^2$
15 ft, 9 ft   20 cm, 12 cm |

Name:	Date: ....

Topic	Mean, Median, Mode, and Range of the Given Data
Notes	✓ Mean: $\frac{sum\ of\ the\ data}{total\ number\ of\ data\ entires}$ ✓ Mode: value in the list that appears most often. ✓ Median: is the middle number of a group of numbers that have been arranged in order by size. ✓ Range: the difference of largest value and smallest value in the list.
Example	***Find the mode and median of these numbers?*** $16, 10, 6, 3, 1, 16, 2, 4$ **Solution:** Mode: value in the list that appears most often. Number 16 is the value in the list that appears most often (there are two number 16). To find median, write the numbers in order: $1, 2, 3, 4, 6, 10, 16, 16$ Number 4 and 6 are in the middle. Find their average: $\frac{4+6}{2} = \frac{10}{2} = 5$ The median is 5.
Your Turn!	1) $3, 2, 4, 8, 3, 10$ Mode: _____ Range: _____ Mean: _____ Median: _____ 2) $6, 3, 2, 9, 5, 7, 2, 14$ Mode: _____ Range: _____ Mean: _____ Median: _____ 3) $5, 4, 3, 2, 9, 5, 6, 8, 12$ Mode: _____ Range: _____ Mean: _____ Median: _____ 4) $12, 6, 8, 6, 9, 6, 4, 13$ Mode: _____ Range: _____ Mean: _____ Median: _____

Name:	Date: ....

Topic	**Mean, Median, Mode, and Range of the Given Data - Answers**
Notes	✓ Mean: $\dfrac{sum\ of\ the\ data}{total\ number\ of\ data\ entires}$ ✓ Mode: value in the list that appears most often. ✓ Median: is the middle number of a group of numbers that have been arranged in order by size. ✓ Range: the difference of largest value and smallest value in the list.
Example	**Find the mode and median of these numbers?** $16, 10, 6, 3, 1, 16, 2, 4$ **Solution:** Mode: value in the list that appears most often. Number 16 is the value in the list that appears most often (there are two number 16). To find median, write the numbers in order: $1, 2, 3, 4, 6, 10, 16, 16$ Number 4 and 6 are in the middle. Find their average: $\dfrac{4+6}{2} = \dfrac{10}{2} = 5$ The median is 5.

Your Turn!	1) $3, 2, 4, 8, 3, 10$ Mode: 3 Range: 8 Mean: 5 Median: 3.5	2) $6, 3, 2, 9, 5, 7, 2, 14$ Mode: 2 Range: 12 Mean: 6 Median: 5.5
	3) $5, 4, 3, 2, 9, 5, 6, 8, 12$ Mode: 5 Range: 10 Mean: 6 Median: 5	4) $12, 6, 8, 6, 9, 6, 4, 13$ Mode: 6 Range: 9 Mean: 8 Median: 7

Name:	Date: ....

Topic	**Probability Problems**
Notes	✓ Probability is the likelihood of something happening in the future. It is expressed as a number between zero (can never happen) to 1 (will always happen). ✓ Probability can be expressed as a fraction, a decimal, or a percent. ✓ Probability formula: $Probability = \frac{number\ of\ desired\ outcomes}{number\ of\ total\ outcomes}$
Example	***If there are 3 green balls, 4 red balls, and 10 blue balls in a basket, what is the probability that Jason will pick out a red ball from the basket?*** **Solution:** There are 4 red ball and 17 are total number of balls. Therefore, probability that Jason will pick out a red ball from the basket is 4 out of 17 or $\frac{4}{3+4+10} = \frac{4}{17}$
Your Turn!	1) A number is chosen at random from 1 to 20. Find the probability of selecting a prime number. (A prime number is a whole number that is only divisible by itself and 1) _____ 2) There are only red and blue cards in a box. The probability of choosing a red card in the box at random is one third. If there are 24 blue cards, how many cards are in the box? _____ 3) A die is rolled, what is the probability that an even number is obtained? _____

Name:	**Date:** ....

Topic	**Probability Problems - Answers**
Notes	✓ Probability is the likelihood of something happening in the future. It is expressed as a number between zero (can never happen) to 1 (will always happen). ✓ Probability can be expressed as a fraction, a decimal, or a percent. ✓ Probability formula: $Probability = \frac{number\ of\ desired\ outcomes}{number\ of\ total\ outcomes}$
Example	***If there are 3 green balls, 4 red balls, and 10 blue balls in a basket, what is the probability that Jason will pick out a red ball from the basket?*** **Solution:** There are 4 red ball and 17 are total number of balls. Therefore, probability that Jason will pick out a red ball from the basket is 4 out of 17 or $\frac{4}{3+4+10} = \frac{4}{17}$
Your Turn!	1) A number is chosen at random from 1 to 20. Find the probability of selecting a prime number. (A prime number is a whole number that is only divisible by itself and 1) $\frac{8}{20} = \frac{2}{5}$ *(There are 8 prime numbers from 1 to 20: 2, 3, 5, 7, 11, 13, 17, 19)*
	2) There are only red and blue cards in a box. The probability of choosing a red card in the box at random is one third. If there are 24 blue cards, how many cards are in the box? 36
	3) A die is rolled, what is the probability that an even number is obtained? $\frac{1}{2}$

Name:	Date: ....

Topic	**Pie Graph**
Notes	✓ A Pie Chart is a circle chart divided into sectors, each sector represents the relative size of each value.
Example	A library has 460 books that include Mathematics, Physics, Chemistry, English and History. Use following graph to answer the question. **What is the number of Physics books?** **Solution:** Number of total books $= 460$ Percent of Physics books $= 25\% = 0.25$ Then, umber of Physics books: $$0.25 \times 460 = 115$$

(Pie chart labeled: History 10%, Mathematics 30%, English 15%, Chemistry 20%, Physics 25%)

Your Turn!	The circle graph below shows all Mr. Smith's expenses for last month. Mr. Smith spent $440 for clothes last month.

(Pie chart labeled: Bills 18%, Foods 25%, Others 23%, Clothes 20%, Books 14% — Mr. Smith's last month expenses)

1) How much did Mr. Smith spend for his Books last month? _____

2) How much did Mr. Smith spend for Bills last month? _____

3) How much did Mr. Smith spend for his foods last month? _____

Name:	**Date:** ....

Topic	**Pie Graph**
Notes	✓ A Pie Chart is a circle chart divided into sectors, each sector represents the relative size of each value.
Example	A library has 460 books that include Mathematics, Physics, Chemistry, English and History. Use following graph to answer the question. **What is the number of Physics books?** **Solution:** Number of total books = 460 Percent of Physics books = 25% = 0.25 Then, umber of Physics books: $$0.25 \times 460 = 115$$ History 10% Mathematics 30% English 15% Chemistry 20% Physics 25%
Your Turn!	The circle graph below shows all Mr. Smith's expenses for last month. Mr. Smith spent $440 for clothes last month. Foods 25% Bills 18% Others 23% Clothes 20% Books 14% Mr. Smith's last month expenses
	1) How much did Mr. Smith spend for his Books last month? $308 2) How much did Mr. Smith spend for Bills last month? $396 3) How much did Mr. Smith spend for his foods last month? $550

Name:	Date: ....

Topic	**Permutations and Combinations**
Notes	✓ Permutations: The number of ways to choose a sample of k elements from a set of n distinct objects where order does matter, and replacements are not allowed. For a permutation problem, use this formula: $$_nP_k = \frac{n!}{(n-k)!}$$ ✓ Combination: The number of ways to choose a sample of r elements from a set of n distinct objects where order does not matter, and replacements are not allowed. For a combination problem, use this formula: $$_nC_r = \frac{n!}{r!\,(n-r)!}$$ ✓ Factorials are products, indicated by an exclamation mark. For example, 4! Equals: $4 \times 3 \times 2 \times 1$. Remember that 0! is defined to be equal to 1.
Example	*How many ways can we pick a team of 4 people from a group of 8?* **Solution:** Since the order doesn't matter, we need to use combination formula where n is 8 and r is 4. Then: $\frac{n!}{r!\,(n-r)!} = \frac{8!}{4!\,(8-4)!} = \frac{8!}{4!\,(4)!} = \frac{8 \times 7 \times 6 \times 5 \times 4!}{4!\,(4)!} = \frac{8 \times 7 \times 6 \times 5}{4 \times 3 \times 2 \times 1} = \frac{1,680}{24} = 70$
Your Turn!	1) In how many ways can 8 athletes be arranged in a straight line? _____
	2) How many ways can we award a first and second place prize among eight contestants? _____
	3) In how many ways can we choose 3 players from a team of 9 players? _____

| Name: .... | Date: .... |

Topic	**Permutations and Combinations - Answers**
Notes	✓ Permutations: The number of ways to choose a sample of k elements from a set of n distinct objects where order does matter, and replacements are not allowed. For a permutation problem, use this formula: $$_nP_k = \frac{n!}{(n-k)!}$$ ✓ Combination: The number of ways to choose a sample of r elements from a set of n distinct objects where order does not matter, and replacements are not allowed. For a combination problem, use this formula: $$_nC_r = \frac{n!}{r!\,(n-r)!}$$ ✓ Factorials are products, indicated by an exclamation mark. For example, 4! Equals: $4 \times 3 \times 2 \times 1$. Remember that 0! is defined to be equal to 1.
Example	*How many ways can we pick a team of 4 people from a group of 8?* **Solution:** Since the order doesn't matter, we need to use combination formula where n is 8 and r is 4. Then: $\frac{n!}{r!\,(n-r)!} = \frac{8!}{4!\,(8-4)!} = \frac{8!}{4!\,(4)!} = \frac{8 \times 7 \times 6 \times 5 \times 4!}{4!\,(4)!} = \frac{8 \times 7 \times 6 \times 5}{4 \times 3 \times 2 \times 1} = \frac{1,680}{24} = 70$
Your Turn!	1) In how many ways can 8 athletes be arranged in a straight line? 40,320
	2) How many ways can we award a first and second place prize among eight contestants? 56
	3) In how many ways can we choose 3 players from a team of 9 players? 84

Name:		Date: ....

Topic	**Function Notation and Evaluation**	
Notes	✓ Functions are mathematical operations that assign unique outputs to given inputs. ✓ Function notation is the way a function is written. It is meant to be a precise way of giving information about the function without a rather lengthy written explanation. ✓ The most popular function notation is $f(x)$ which is read "f of x". ✓ To evaluate a function, plug in the input (the given value or expression) for the function's variable (place holder, x).	
Example	**Evaluate**: $h(n) = 2n^2 - 2$, find $h(2)$. **Solution:** Substitute n with 2: Then: $h(n) = 2n^2 - 2 \rightarrow h(2) = 2(2)^2 - 2 = 8 - 2 \rightarrow h(2) = 6$	
Your Turn!	1) $f(x) = x - 2$, find $f(-1)$ _____	2) $g(x) = 2x + 4$, find $g(3)$ _____
	3) $g(n) = 2n - 8$, find $g(-1)$ _____	4) $h(n) = n^2 - 1$, find $h(-2)$ _____
	5) $f(x) = x^2 + 12$, find $f(5)$ _____	6) $g(x) = 2x^2 - 9$, find $g(-2)$ _____
	7) $w(x) = 2x^2 - 4x$, find $w(2n)$ _____	8) $p(x) = 4x^3 - 10$, find $p(-3a)$ _____

| Name: .... | Date: .... |

Topic	**Function Notation and Evaluation - Answers**	
Notes	✓ Functions are mathematical operations that assign unique outputs to given inputs. ✓ Function notation is the way a function is written. It is meant to be a precise way of giving information about the function without a rather lengthy written explanation. ✓ The most popular function notation is $f(x)$ which is read "f of x". ✓ To evaluate a function, plug in the input (the given value or expression) for the function's variable (place holder, x).	
Example	**Evaluate**: $h(n) = 2n^2 - 2$, find $h(2)$. **Solution:** Substitute n with 2: Then: $h(n) = 2n^2 - 2 \rightarrow h(2) = 2(2)^2 - 2 = 8 - 2 \rightarrow h(2) = 6$	

Your Turn!	1) $f(x) = x - 2$, find $f(-1)$ $f(-1) = -3$	2) $g(x) = 2x + 4$, find $g(3)$ $g(3) = 10$
	3) $g(n) = 2n - 8$, find $g(-1)$ $g(-1) = -10$	4) $h(n) = n^2 - 1$, find $h(-2)$ $h(-2) = 3$
	5) $f(x) = x^2 + 12$, find $f(5)$ $f(5) = 37$	6) $g(x) = 2x^2 - 9$, find $g(-2)$ $g(-2) = -1$
	7) $w(x) = 2x^2 - 4x$, find $w(2n)$ $w(2n) = 8n^2 - 8n$	8) $p(x) = 4x^3 - 10$, find $p(-3a)$ $p(-3a) = -108a^3 + 30a$

Name:	Date: ....

Topic	Adding and Subtracting Functions
Notes	✓ Just like we can add and subtract numbers and expressions, we can add or subtract two functions and simplify or evaluate them. The result is a new function. ✓ For two functions $f(x)$ and $g(x)$, we can create two new functions: $(f + g)(x) = f(x) + g(x)$ and $(f - g)(x) = f(x) - g(x)$
Example	$g(a) = 2a - 5, f(a) = a + 8$, Find: $(g + f)(a)$ **Solution:** $(g + f)(a) = g(a) + f(a)$ Then: $(g + f)(a) = (2a - 5) + (a + 8) = 3a + 3$

Your Turn!	1) $g(x) = x - 2$ $h(x) = 2x + 6$ Find: $(h + g)(3)$ _____	2) $f(x) = 3x + 2$ $g(x) = -x - 6$ Find: $(f + g)(2)$ _____
	3) $f(x) = 5x + 8$ $g(x) = 3x - 12$ Find: $(f - g)(-2)$ _____	4) $h(x) = 2x^2 - 10$ $g(x) = 3x + 12$ Find: $(h + g)(3)$ _____
	5) $g(x) = 12x - 8$ $h(x) = 3x^2 + 14$ Find: $(h - g)(x)$ _____	6) $h(x) = -2x^2 - 18$ $g(x) = 4x^2 + 15$ Find: $(h - g)(a)$ _____

Name: ....

Date: ....

Topic	Adding and Subtracting Functions - Answers
Notes	✓ Just like we can add and subtract numbers and expressions, we can add or subtract two functions and simplify or evaluate them. The result is a new function. ✓ For two functions $f(x)$ and $g(x)$, we can create two new functions: $(f + g)(x) = f(x) + g(x)$ and $(f - g)(x) = f(x) - g(x)$
Example	$g(a) = 2a - 5, f(a) = a + 8$, Find: $(g + f)(a)$ **Solution:** $(g + f)(a) = g(a) + f(a)$ Then: $(g + f)(a) = (2a - 5) + (a + 8) = 3a + 3$
Your Turn!	1) $g(x) = x - 2$ $h(x) = 2x + 6$ Find: $(h + g)(3)$ 13 2) $f(x) = 3x + 2$ $g(x) = -x - 6$ Find: $(f + g)(2)$ 0
	3) $f(x) = 5x + 8$ $g(x) = 3x - 12$ Find: $(f - g)(-2)$ 16 4) $h(x) = 2x^2 - 10$ $g(x) = 3x + 12$ Find: $(h + g)(3)$ 29
	5) $g(x) = 12x - 8$ $h(x) = 3x^2 + 14$ Find: $(h - g)(x)$ $3x^2 - 12x + 22$ 6) $h(x) = -2x^2 - 18$ $g(x) = 4x^2 + 15$ Find: $(h - g)(a)$ $-6a^2 - 33$

Name:	Date: ....

Topic	**Multiplying and Dividing Functions**
Notes	✓ Just like we can multiply and divide numbers and expressions, we can multiply and divide two functions and simplify or evaluate them. ✓ For two functions $f(x)$ and $g(x)$, we can create two new functions: $(f.g)(x) = f(x).g(x)$ and $\left(\frac{f}{g}\right)(x) = \frac{f(x)}{g(x)}$
Example	$g(x) = x + 5$, $f(x) = x - 3$, Find: $(g.f)(2)$ **Solution:** $(g.f)(x) = g(x).f(x) = (x+5)(x-3) = x^2 - 3x + 5x - 15 = x^2 + 2x - 15$ Substitute x with 2: $(g.f)(x) = (2)^2 + 2(2) - 15 = 4 + 4 - 15 = -7$

Your Turn!	1) $g(x) = x - 5$ $h(x) = x + 6$ Find: $(g.h)(-1)$ _____	2) $f(x) = 2x + 2$ $g(x) = -x - 6$ Find: $(\frac{f}{g})(-2)$ _____
	3) $f(x) = 5x + 3$ $g(x) = 2x - 4$ Find: $(\frac{f}{g})(5)$ _____	4) $h(x) = x^2 - 2$ $g(x) = x + 4$ Find: $(g.h)(3)$ _____
	5) $g(x) = 4x - 12$ $h(x) = x^2 + 4$ Find: $(g.h)(-2)$ _____	6) $h(x) = 3x^2 - 8$ $g(x) = 4x + 6$ Find: $(\frac{f}{g})(-4)$ _____

Name:	Date: ....

Topic	**Multiplying and Dividing Functions - Answers**	
Notes	✓ Just like we can multiply and divide numbers and expressions, we can multiply and divide two functions and simplify or evaluate them. ✓ For two functions $f(x)$ and $g(x)$, we can create two new functions: $(f.g)(x) = f(x).g(x)$ and $\left(\frac{f}{g}\right)(x) = \frac{f(x)}{g(x)}$	
Example	$g(x) = x + 5, f(x) = x - 3$, Find: $(g.f)(2)$ **Solution:** $(g.f)(x) = g(x).f(x) = (x + 5)(x - 3) = x^2 - 3x + 5x - 15 = x^2 + 2x - 15$ Substitute x with 2: $(g.f)(x) = (2)^2 + 2(2) - 15 = 4 + 4 - 15 = -7$	
Your Turn!	1) $g(x) = x - 5$ $h(x) = x + 6$ Find: $(g.h)(-1)$ $(g.h)(-1) = -30$	2) $f(x) = 2x + 2$ $g(x) = -x - 6$ Find: $(\frac{f}{g})(-2)$ $\left(\frac{f}{g}\right)(-2) = \frac{1}{2}$
	3) $f(x) = 5x + 3$ $g(x) = 2x - 4$ Find: $(\frac{f}{g})(5)$ $\left(\frac{f}{g}\right)(5) = \frac{14}{3}$	4) $h(x) = x^2 - 2$ $g(x) = x + 4$ Find: $(g.h)(3)$ $(g.h)(3) = 49$
	5) $g(x) = 4x - 12$ $h(x) = x^2 + 4$ Find: $(g.h)(-2)$ $(g.h)(-2) = -160$	6) $h(x) = 3x^2 - 8$ $g(x) = 4x + 6$ Find: $(\frac{f}{g})(-4)$ $\left(\frac{f}{g}\right)(-4) = -4$

Name:	Date: ....

Topic	Composition of Functions	
Notes	✓ "Composition of functions" simply means combining two or more functions in a way where the output from one function becomes the input for the next function. ✓ The notation used for composition is: $(fog)(x) = f(g(x))$ and is read "f composed with g of x" or "f of g of x".	
Example	**Using** $f(x) = x - 8$ **and** $g(x) = x + 2$, **find:** $(f \circ g)(3)$ **Solution:** $(f \circ g)(x) = f(g(x))$ *Then:* $(f \circ g)(x) = f(g(x)) = f(x + 2) = x + 2 - 8 = x - 6$ Substitute x with 3: $(f \circ g)(3) = f(g(3)) = 3 - 6 = -3$	
Your Turn!	1) $f(x) = 2x$ $g(x) = x + 3$ Find: $(fog)(2)$ _____	2) $f(x) = x + 2$ $g(x) = x - 6$ Find: $(fog)(-1)$ _____
	3) $f(x) = 3x$ $g(x) = x + 4$ Find: $(gof)(4)$ _____	4) $h(x) = 2x - 2$ $g(x) = x + 4$ Find: $(goh)(2)$ _____
	5) $f(x) = 2x - 8$ $g(x) = x + 10$ Find: $(fog)(-2)$ _____	6) $f(x) = x^2 - 8$ $g(x) = 2x + 3$ Find: $(gof)(4)$ _____

Name:		Date: ....

Topic	Composition of Functions - Answers	
Notes	✓ "Composition of functions" simply means combining two or more functions in a way where the output from one function becomes the input for the next function. ✓ The notation used for composition is: $(fog)(x) = f(g(x))$ and is read "f composed with g of x" or "f of g of x".	
Example	*Using* $f(x) = x - 8$ *and* $g(x) = x + 2$, *find:* $(f \circ g)(3)$ **Solution:** $(f \circ g)(x) = f(g(x))$ *Then:* $(f \circ g)(x) = f(g(x)) = f(x + 2) = x + 2 - 8 = x - 6$ Substitute x with 3: $(f \circ g)(3) = f(g(3)) = 3 - 6 = -3$	
Your Turn!	1) $f(x) = 2x$ $g(x) = x + 3$ Find: $(fog)(2)$ 10	2) $f(x) = x + 2$ $g(x) = x - 6$ Find: $(fog)(-1)$ -5
	3) $f(x) = 3x$ $g(x) = x + 4$ Find: $(gof)(4)$ 16	4) $h(x) = 2x - 2$ $g(x) = x + 4$ Find: $(goh)(2)$ 6
	5) $f(x) = 2x - 8$ $g(x) = x + 10$ Find: $(fog)(-2)$ 8	6) $f(x) = x^2 - 8$ $g(x) = 2x + 3$ Find: $(gof)(4)$ 19

GED Test Review

The General Educational Development Test, commonly known as the GED or high school equivalency degree, is a standardized test and is the only high school equivalency test recognized in all 50 USA states.

Currently, GED is a computer-based test. Official computer-based tests are given at test centers all over the country. There are four subject area tests on GED:

- o Reasoning Through Language Arts,
- o Mathematical Reasoning,
- o Social Studies,
- o Science

The GED Mathematical Reasoning test is a 115-minute, single-section test that covers basic mathematics topics, quantitative problem-solving and algebraic questions. There are two parts on Mathematical Reasoning section. The first part contains 5 questions where calculators are not permitted. The second part contains 41 test questions. Calculator is allowed in the second part.

In this book, there are 2 complete GED Mathematical Reasoning Tests. Take these tests to see what score you'll be able to receive on a real GED test.

Good luck!

Time to refine your skill with a practice examination

Take a practice GED Math Test to simulate the test day experience. After you've finished, score your test using the answer key.

Before You Start

- You'll need a pencil and a calculator to take the test.

- There are two types of questions:

  Multiple choice questions: for each of these questions, there are four or more possible answers. Choose which one is best.

  Grid-ins questions: for these questions, write your answer in the box provided.

- It's okay to guess. You won't lose any points if you're wrong.

- The GED® Mathematical Reasoning test contains a formula sheet, which displays formulas relating to geometric measurement and certain algebra concepts. Formulas are provided to test- takers so that they may focus on application, rather than the memorization, of formulas.

- After you've finished the test, review the answer key to see where you went wrong and what areas you need to improve.

Good luck!

GED Mathematical Reasoning

Practice Test 1

2020-2021

Two Parts

Total number of questions: 46

Part 1 (Non-Calculator): 5 questions

Part 2 (Calculator): 41 questions

Total time for two parts: 115 Minutes

GED Test Mathematics Formula Sheet

Area of a:

Parallelogram

Trapezoid

$$A = bh$$

$$A = \frac{1}{2}h(b_1 + b_2)$$

Surface Area and Volume of a:

Rectangular/Right Prism

Cylinder

Pyramid

Cone

Sphere

$$SA = ph + 2B \qquad\qquad V = Bh$$

$$SA = 2\pi rh + 2\pi r^2 \qquad V = \pi r^2 h$$

$$SA = \frac{1}{2}ps + B \qquad\qquad V = \frac{1}{3}Bh$$

$$SA = \pi r + \pi r^2 \qquad\qquad V = \frac{1}{3}\pi r^2 h$$

$$SA = 4\pi r^2 \qquad\qquad V = \frac{4}{3}\pi r^3$$

(*p* = perimeter of base *B*; π = 3.14)

Algebra

Slope of a line

$$m = \frac{y_2 - y_1}{x_2 - x_1}$$

Slope-intercept form of the equation of
a line

$$y = mx + b$$

Point-slope form of the Equation of a
line

$$y - y_1 = m(x - x_1)$$

Standard form of a Quadratic equation

$$y = ax^2 + bx + c$$

Quadratic formula

$$x = \frac{-b \pm \sqrt{b^2 - 4ac}}{2a}$$

Pythagorean theorem

$$a^2 + b^2 = c^2$$

Simple interest

$$I = prt$$

(*I* = interest, *p* = principal, *r* = rate, *t* = time)

GED Mathematical Reasoning

Practice Test 1

Part 1 (Non-Calculator)

5 questions

Total time for two parts (Non-Calculator, and Calculator parts): 115 Minutes

You may **NOT** use a calculator on this part.

1) If $3x - 5 = 8.5$, what is the value of $6x + 3$?

   ☐A. 13

   ☐C. 20.5

   ☐B. 15.5

   ☐D. 30

2) What is the area of an isosceles right triangle that has one leg that measures $8\ cm$?

   ☐A. $6\ cm^2$

   ☐C. $18\ cm^2$

   ☐B. $12\ cm^2$

   ☐D. $32\ cm^2$

3) A shirt costing $600 is discounted 25%. After a month, the shirt is discounted another 15%. Which of the following expressions can be used to find the selling price of the shirt?

   ☐A. $(600)(0.60)$

   ☐C. $(600)(0.25) - (200)(0.15)$

   ☐B. $(600) - 600\ (0.40)$

   ☐D. $(600)(0.75)(0.85)$

4) Which of the following points lies on the line with equation $3x + 5y = 11$?

   ☐A. $(2, 1)$

   ☐C. $(-2, 2)$

   ☐B. $(-1, 2)$

   ☐D. $(2, 2)$

5) What is the value of expression? $-15 + 6 \times (-5) - [4 + 22 \times (-4)] \div 2 = ?$

   Write your answer in the box below.

   ☐

GED Mathematical Reasoning

Practice Test 1

Part 2 (Calculator)

41 questions

Total time for two parts (Non-Calculator, and Calculator parts): 115 Minutes

You may use a calculator on this part.

1) The average of five consecutive numbers is 40. What is the smallest number?

   ☐A. 38   ☐B. 36

   ☐C. 34   ☐D. 12

2) How many tiles of $8\ cm^2$ is needed to cover a floor of dimension $7\ cm$ by $24\ cm$?

   ☐A. 6   ☐B. 12

   ☐C. 21   ☐D. 24

3) A rope weighs 600 grams per meter of length. What is the weight in kilograms of 15.2 meters of this rope? ($1\ kilograms\ =\ 1,000\ grams$)

   ☐A. 0.0912   ☐B. 0.912

   ☐C. 9.12   ☐D. 91.20

4) A chemical solution contains 6% alcohol. If there is $24\ ml$ of alcohol, what is the volume of the solution?

   ☐A. $240\ ml$ ☐B. $400\ ml$

   ☐C. $600\ ml$ ☐D. $1200\ ml$

5) The average weight of 18 girls in a class is $60\ kg$ and the average weight of 32 boys in the same class is $62\ kg$. What is the average weight of all the 50 students in that class?

   ☐A. 60   ☐B. 61.28

   ☐C. 61.68   ☐D. 62.90

6) The price of a laptop is decreased by 10% to $360. What is its original price?

☐A. $320   ☐B. $380

☐C. $400   ☐D. $450

7) What is the median of these numbers? $4, 9, 13, 8, 15, 18, 5$

☐A. 8   ☐B. 9

☐C. 13   ☐D. 15

8) The radius of the following cylinder is 8 inches and its height is 16 inches. What is the surface area of the cylinder in square inches?

Write your answer in the box below. (π equals 3.14)

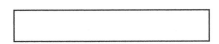

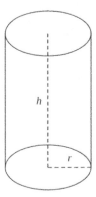

9) In 1999, the average worker's income increased $2,000 per year starting from $27,000 annual salary. Which equation represents income greater than average? (I = income, x = number of years after 1999)

☐A. $I > 2,000\,x + 27,000$ ☐B. $I > -2,000\,x + 27,000$

☐C. $I < -2,000\,x + 27,000$ ☐D. $I < 2,000\,x - 27,000$

10) What is the value of y in the following system of equation?

$$3x - 4y = -20$$

$$-x + 2y = 10$$

Write your answer in the box below.

11) What is the area of a square whose diagonal is 6 meters?

☐ A. 20 m^2 ☐ C. 12 m^2

☐ B. 18 m^2 ☐ D. 10 m^2

12) The width of a box is one third of its length. The height of the box is half of its width. If the length of the box is 24 cm, what is the volume of the box?

☐ A. 81 cm^3 ☐ B. 162 cm^3

☐ C. 243 cm^3 ☐ D. 768 cm^3

13) If 60% of A is 20% of B, then B is what percent of A?

☐ A. 3%   ☐ B. 30%

☐ C. 200%   ☐ D. 300%

14) How many possible outfit combination come from six shirts, three slacks, and six ties?

Write your answer in the box below.

15) A bank is offering 2.5% simple interest on a savings account. If you deposit $8,000, how much interest will you earn in five years?

☐A. $360   ☐B. $720

☐C. $1,000   ☐D. $3,600

16) What is the value of 6^5 ?

Write your answer in the box below.

17) 15 is What percent of 20?

☐A. 20%   ☐B. 75%

☐C. 125%   ☐D. 150%

18) The perimeter of the trapezoid below is 50. What is its area?

Write your answer in the box below.

19) In five successive hours, a car travels $40\ km$, $45\ km$, $50\ km$, $35\ km$ and $55\ km$. In the next five hours, it travels with an average speed of $45\ km\ per\ hour$. Find the total distance the car traveled in $10\ hours$.

☐A. $425\ km$ ☐B. $450\ km$

☐C. $475\ km$ ☐D. $500\ km$

20) How long does a 420– *miles* trip take moving at 60 *miles per hour* (*mph*)?

☐A. 4 *hours*   ☐B. 7 *hours*

☐C. 7 *hours and* 24 *minutes*   ☐D. 8 *hours and* 10 *minutes*

21) Which of the following points lies on the line $4x + 6y = 20$?

☐A. $(2, 1)$ ☐B. $(-1, 3)$

☐C. $(-2, 2)$ ☐D. $(2, 2)$

22) Two third of 15 is equal to $\frac{2}{5}$ of what number?

☐A. 12   ☐B. 20

☐C. 25   ☐D. 60

23) The marked price of a computer is D dollar. Its price decreased by 20% in January and later increased by 15% in February. What is the final price of the computer in D dollar?

☐A. 0.80 D ☐B. 0.88 D

☐C. 0.92 D ☐D. 1.20

24) A $45 shirt now selling for $28 is discounted by about what percent?

☐A. 20%   ☐B. 37.7%

☐C. 40%   ☐D. 60%

25) Which of the following could be the product of two consecutive prime numbers? (Select one or more answer choices)

☐A. 2   ☐B. 10

☐C. 14   ☐D. 15

☐E. 35

26) The ratio of boys to girls in a school is $2:3$. If there are 400 students in a school, how many boys are in the school.

Write your answer in the box below.

```
┌─────────────────────────┐
│                         │
│                         │
└─────────────────────────┘
```

27) Sophia purchased a sofa for \$530.40. The sofa is regularly priced at \$631. What was the percent discount Sophia received on the sofa?

☐A. 12%   ☐B. 16%

☐C. 20%   ☐D. 25%

28) The score of Emma was half as that of Ava and the score of Mia was twice that of Ava. If the score of Mia was 60, what is the score of Emma?

☐A. 12   ☐B. 15

☐C. 20   ☐D. 30

29) A bag contains 21 balls: two green, six black, eight blue, two brown, two red and one white. If 20 balls are removed from the bag at random, what is the probability that a white ball has been removed?

☐A. $\frac{1}{9}$ ☐B. $\frac{1}{6}$

☐C. $\frac{4}{5}$ ☐D. $\frac{20}{21}$

30) A taxi driver earns \$8 per 1-hour work. If he works 10 hours a day and in 1 hour he uses 2-liters petrol with price \$1 for 1-liter. How much money does he earn in one day?

☐A. \$90   ☐B. \$88

☐C. \$70   ☐D. \$60

31) The average of 13, 15, 20 and x is 25. What is the value of x?

Write your answer in the box below.

┌─────────────────────┐
│   │
└─────────────────────┘

32) The price of a sofa is decreased by 15% to $476. What was its original price?

☐A. $480   ☐B. $520

☐C. $560   ☐D. $600

33) When a number is subtracted from 28 and the difference is divided by that number, the result is 3. What is the value of the number?

☐A. 2   ☐B. 4

☐C. 7   ☐D. 12

34) An angle is equal to one fourth of its supplement. What is the measure of that angle?

☐A.18   ☐B. 24

☐ C. 36   ☐D. 45

35) John traveled 150 km in 6 hours and Alice traveled 160 km in 4 hours. What is the ratio of the average speed of John to average speed of Alice?

☐A. 3 : 2   ☐B. 2 : 3

☐C. 5 : 8   ☐D. 5 : 6

36) Right triangle ABC has two legs of lengths 5 cm (AB) and 12 cm (AC). What is the length of the third side (BC)?

☐ A. 6 cm ☐ B. 8 cm

☐ C. 13 cm ☐ D. 15 cm

37) If 75% of a class are girls, and $\frac{1}{3}$ of girls take drawing class this semester, what percent of the class are girls who take drawing class this semester?

☐A. 25%   ☐B. 28%

☐C. 35%   ☐D. 37.5%

38) The area of a circle is less than 49π. Which of the following can be the circumference of the circle? (Select one or more answer choices)

☒A. 8π ☐C. 14π ☐E. 49π

☐B. 12π ☐D. 32π

39) If $2y + 6 < 30$, then y could be equal to? (Select one or more answer choices)

☐A. 15   ☐C. 12   ☐E. -12

☐B. 14   ☐D. 8

40) From last year, the price of a table has increased from $125.00 to $185.00. The new price is what percent of the original price?

☐A. 72%   ☐B. 120%

☐C. 148%   ☐D. 160%

41) A boat sails 80 *miles* south and then 150 *miles* east. How far is the boat from its start point?

☐A. 160 *miles*   ☐B. 170 *miles*

☐C. 200 *miles*   ☐D. 230 *miles*

End of GED Mathematical Reasoning Practice Test 1.

GED Mathematical Reasoning

Practice Test 2

2020-2021

Two Parts

Total number of questions: 46

Part 1 (Non-Calculator): 5 questions

Part 2 (Calculator): 41 questions

Total time for two parts: 115 Minutes

GED Test Mathematics Formula Sheet

Area of a:

Parallelogram

$$A = bh$$

Trapezoid

$$A = \frac{1}{2}h(b_1 + b_2)$$

Surface Area and Volume of a:

Rectangular/Right Prism

Cylinder

Pyramid

Cone

Sphere

$$SA = ph + 2B \qquad\qquad V = Bh$$
$$SA = 2\pi rh + 2\pi r^2 \qquad V = \pi r^2 h$$
$$SA = \frac{1}{2}ps + B \qquad\quad V = \frac{1}{3}Bh$$
$$SA = \pi r + \pi r^2 \qquad\quad V = \frac{1}{3}\pi r^2 h$$
$$SA = 4\pi r^2 \qquad\qquad V = \frac{4}{3}\pi r^3$$

(p = perimeter of base B; $\pi = 3.14$)

Algebra

Slope of a line

$$m = \frac{y_2 - y_1}{x_2 - x_1}$$

Slope-intercept form of the equation of a line

$$y = mx + b$$

Point-slope form of the Equation of a line

$$y - y_1 = m(x - x_1)$$

Standard form of a Quadratic equation

$$y = ax^2 + bx + c$$

Quadratic formula

$$x = \frac{-b \pm \sqrt{b^2 - 4ac}}{2a}$$

Pythagorean theorem

$$a^2 + b^2 = c^2$$

Simple interest

$$I = prt$$

(I = interest, p = principal, r = rate, t = time)

GED Mathematical Reasoning

Practice Test 2

Part 1 (Non-Calculator)

5 questions

Total time for two parts (Non-Calculator, and Calculator parts): 115 Minutes

You may NOT use a calculator on this part.

1) What is the value of this expression? $[3 \times (-14) - 48] - (-14) + [3 \times 8] \div 2$

Write your answer in the box below.

2) A tree 32 feet tall casts a shadow 12 feet long. Jack is 6 feet tall. How long is Jack's shadow?

☐A. 2.25 ft ☐B. 4 ft

☐C. 4.25 ft ☐D. 8 ft

3) What is the product of all possible values of x in the following equation?

$$|2x - 6| = 12$$

☐A. −27   ☐B. −3

☐C. 9   ☐D. 27

4) What is the slope of a line that is perpendicular to the line $3x - y = 6$?

☐A. −3   ☐B. $-\frac{1}{3}$

☐C. 2   ☐D. 6

5) What is the value of the expression $3(x - 2y) + (2 - x)^2$ when $x = 5$ and $= -3$?

☐A. −22   ☐B. 24

☐C. 42   ☐D. 88

GED Mathematical Reasoning

Practice Test 2

Part 2 (Calculator)

41 questions

Total time for two parts (Non-Calculator, and Calculator parts): 115 Minutes

You may use a calculator on this part.

1) If $x - 4(x + 2) = -15.5$, what is the value of x?

   Write your answer in the box below.

   ┌─────────────────────┐
   │   │
   └─────────────────────┘

2) Which of the following answers represents the compound inequality $-4 \leq 4x - 8 < 16$?

   ☐A. $-2 \leq x \leq 8$ ☐C. $1 < x \leq 6$

   ☐B. $-2 < x \leq 8$ ☐D. $1 \leq x < 6$

3) What is the volume of a box with the following dimensions?

   Hight = 4 cm Width = 5 cm Length = 6 cm

   ☐A. $15\ cm^3$ ☐B. $60\ cm^3$

   ☐C. $90\ cm^3$ ☐D. $120\ cm^3$

4) Simplify the expression.

   $$(6x^3 - 8x^2 + 2x^4) - (4x^2 - 2x^4 + 2x^3)$$

   ☐A. $4x^4 + 4x^3 - 12x^2$ ☐B. $4x^3 - 12x^2$

   ☐C. $4x^4 + 4x^3 + 12x^2$ ☐D. $8x^3 - 12x^2$

5) In two successive years, the population of a town is increased by 15% and 20%. What percent of the population is increased after two years?

   ☐A. 32%   ☐B. 35%

   ☐C. 38%   ☐D. 68%

6) Last week 24,000 fans attended a football match. This week three times as many bought tickets, but one sixth of them cancelled their tickets. How many are attending this week?

☐A. 48,000   ☐B. 54,000

☐C. 60,000   ☐D. 72,000

7) What is the perimeter of a square in centimeters that has an area of 595.36 cm^2?

Write your answer in the box below. (don't write the measurement)

8) Which of the following shows the numbers from least to greatest?

☐ A. $67\%, 0.68, \frac{2}{3}, \frac{4}{5}$ ☐B. $67\%, 0.68, \frac{4}{5}, \frac{2}{3}$

☐C. $0.68, 67\%, \frac{2}{3}, \frac{4}{5}$ ☐D. $\frac{2}{3}, 67\%, 0.68, \frac{4}{5}$

9) The mean of 50 test scores was calculated as 88. But, it turned out that one of the scores was misread as 94 but it was 69. What is the correct mean of the test scores?

☐A. 85   ☐B. 87

☐C. 87.5   ☐D. 88.5

10) Two dice are thrown simultaneously, what is the probability of getting a sum of 5 or 8?

☐A. $\frac{1}{3}$ ☐B. $\frac{1}{4}$

☐C. $\frac{1}{16}$ ☐D. $\frac{11}{36}$

11) A swimming pool holds 2,000 cubic feet of water. The swimming pool is 25 feet long and 10 feet wide. How deep is the swimming pool?

Write your answer in the box below. (<u>Don't write the measurement</u>)

12) Mr. Carlos family are choosing a menu for their reception. They have 3 choices of appetizers, 5 choices of entrees, 4 choices of cake. How many different menu combinations are possible for them to choose?

☐A. 12   ☐B. 32

☐C. 60   ☐D. 120

13) In a stadium the ratio of home fans to visiting fans in a crowd is $5:7$. Which of the following could be the total number of fans in the stadium? (Select one or more answer choices)

☐A. 12,324   ☐C. 42,326

☐B. 16,788   ☐D. 44,566

☐E. 66,812

14) What is the area of a square whose diagonal is 8?

☐A. 16   ☐B. 32

☐C. 36   ☐D. 64

15) Anita's trick–or–treat bag contains 12 pieces of chocolate, 18 suckers, 18 pieces of gum, 24 pieces of licorice. If she randomly pulls a piece of candy from her bag, what is the probability of her pulling out a piece of sucker?

☐A. $\frac{1}{3}$ ☐B. $\frac{1}{4}$

☐C. $\frac{1}{6}$ ☐D. $\frac{1}{12}$

16) Which of the following points lies on the line $x + 2y = 4$? (Select one or more answer choices)

☐A. $(-2, 3)$ ☐B. $(1, 2)$

☐C. $(-1, 3)$ ☐D. $(-3, 4)$

☐E. $(0, 2)$

17) The perimeter of a rectangular yard is 60 meters. What is its length if its width is twice its length?

☐A. 10 meters   ☐B. 18 meters

☐C. 20 meters   ☐D. 24 meters

18) The average of 6 numbers is 12. The average of 4 of those numbers is 10. What is the average of the other two numbers.

☐A. 10   ☐B. 12

☐C. 14   ☐D. 16

19) What is the value of x in the following system of equations?

$$2x + 5y = 11$$
$$4x - 2y = -14$$

☐A. -1 ☐B. 1

☐C. -2 ☐D. 4

20) The perimeter of the trapezoid below is $36\ cm$. What is its area?

☐A. $576\ cm^2$ ☐B. $70\ cm^2$

☐C. $48\ cm^2$ ☐D. $24\ cm^2$ 6 cm

12 cm   8 cm

21) A card is drawn at random from a standard 52–card deck, what is the probability that the card is of Hearts? (The deck includes 13 of each suit clubs, diamonds, hearts, and spades)

☐A. $\frac{1}{3}$ ☐B. $\frac{1}{4}$

☐C. $\frac{1}{6}$ ☐D. $\frac{1}{52}$

22) The average of five numbers is 25. If a sixth number that is greater than 42 is added, then, which of the following could be the new average? (Select one or more answer choices)

☐A. 25   ☐C. 27

☐B. 26   ☐D. 28

☐E. 42

23) The diagonal of a rectangle is 10 inches long and the height of the rectangle is 8 inches. What is the perimeter of the rectangle in inches?

Write your answer in the box below.

24) The ratio of boys and girls in a class is 4: 7. If there are 44 students in the class, how many more boys should be enrolled to make the ratio 1: 1?

☐A. 8   ☐B. 10

☐C. 12   ☐D. 14

25) Mr. Jones saves $2,500 out of his monthly family income of $55,000. What fractional part of his income does he save?

☐A. $\frac{1}{22}$ ☐B. $\frac{1}{11}$

☐C. $\frac{3}{25}$ ☐D. $\frac{2}{15}$

26) Jason needs an 75% average in his writing class to pass. On his first 4 exams, he earned scores of 68%, 72%, 85%, and 90%. What is the minimum score Jason can earn on his fifth and final test to pass?

Write your answer in the box below.

27) What is the value of x in the following equation? $\frac{2}{3}x + \frac{1}{6} = \frac{1}{3}$

☐A. 6

☐B. $\frac{1}{2}$

☐C. $\frac{1}{3}$

☐D. $\frac{1}{4}$

28) A bank is offering 3.5% simple interest on a savings account. If you deposit $12,000, how much interest will you earn in two years?

☐A. $420

☐B. $840

☐C. $4200

☐D. $8,400

29) Simplify $6x^2y^3(2x^2y)^3 =$

☐A. $12x^4y^6$

☐B. $12x^8y^6$

☐C. $48x^4y^6$

☐D. $48x^8y^6$

30) What is the surface area of the cylinder below?

☐A. $48\,\pi\,in^2$

☐B. $57\,\pi\,in^2$

☐C. $66\,\pi\,in^2$

☐D. $288\,\pi\,in^2$

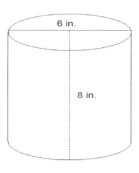

6 in.

8 in.

31) The square of a number is $\frac{25}{64}$. What is the cube of that number?

☐A. $\frac{5}{8}$

☐B. $\frac{25}{254}$

☐C. $\frac{125}{512}$

☐D. $\frac{125}{64}$

32) What is the median of these numbers? 2, 27, 28, 19, 67, 44, 35

☐A. 19 ☐B. 28

☐C. 44 ☐D. 35

33) A cruise line ship left Port A and traveled 80 miles due west and then 150 miles due north. At this point, what is the shortest distance from the cruise to port A in miles?

Write your answer in the box below.

34) What is the equivalent temperature of $104°F$ in Celsius? $C = \frac{5}{9}(F - 32)$

☐A. 32 ☐B. 40

☐C. 48 ☐D. 52

35) If 40% of a number is 4, what is the number?

☐A. 4 ☐B. 8

☐C. 10 ☐D. 12

36) The circle graph below shows all Mr. Green's expenses for last month. If he spent $660 on his car, how much did he spend for his rent?

☐A. $700 ☐B. $740

☐C. $780 ☐D. $810

Mr. Green's monthly expenses

170

37) Jason is 9 miles ahead of Joe running at 5.5 miles per hour and Joe is running at the speed of 7 miles per hour. How long does it take Joe to catch Jason?

☐A. 3 *hours*　　　　　　☐B. 4 *hours*

☐C. 6 *hours*　　　　　　☐D. 8 *hours*

38) 55 students took an exam and 11 of them failed. What percent of the students passed the exam?

☐A. 20%　　　　　　☐B. 40%

☐C. 60%　　　　　　☐D. 80%

39) If 150% of a number is 75, then what is the 90% of that number?

☐A. 45　　　　　　☐B. 50

☐C. 70　　　　　　☐D.85

40) What is the slope of the line? $4x - 2y = 6$

Write your answer in the box below.

┌─────────────────────┐
│   │
└─────────────────────┘

41) A football team had $20,000 to spend on supplies. The team spent $14,000 on new balls. New sport shoes cost $120 each. Which of the following inequalities represent the number of new shoes the team can purchase.

☐A. $120x + 14,000 \leq 20,000$　　　　☐B. $120x + 14,000 \geq 20,000$

☐C. $14,000x + 120 \leq 20,000$　　　　☐D. $14,000x + 12,0 \geq 20,000$

End of GED Mathematical Reasoning Practice Test 2.

GED Mathematical Reasoning Practice Tests

Answer Keys

Now, it's time to review your results to see where you went wrong and what areas you need to improve.

GED Math Practice Test 1						GED Math Practice Test 2					
1	D	**21**	7,776	**41**	C	**1**	−64	**21**	A, E	**41**	D
2	D	**22**	B	**42**	A	**2**	A	**22**	A	**42**	C
3	D	**23**	78	**43**	A, B	**3**	A	**23**	D	**43**	D
4	A	**24**	B	**44**	D, E	**4**	B	**24**	C	**44**	A
5	−3	**25**	B	**45**	C	**5**	C	**25**	B	**45**	2
6	A	**26**	D	**46**	B	**6**	2.5	**26**	B	**46**	A
7	C	**27**	C			**7**	D	**27**	D, E		
8	C	**28**	C			**8**	D	**28**	28		
9	B	**29**	B			**9**	A	**29**	C		
10	B	**30**	D, E			**10**	C	**30**	A		
11	C	**31**	160			**11**	C	**31**	60		
12	B	**32**	B			**12**	97.6	**32**	D		
13	1,205.76	**33**	B			**13**	D	**33**	B		
14	A	**34**	D			**14**	C	**34**	D		
15	5	**35**	D			**15**	B	**35**	C		
16	B	**36**	52			**16**	8	**36**	C		
17	D	**37**	C			**17**	C	**37**	B		
18	D	**38**	C			**18**	A, B	**38**	170		
19	108	**39**	C			**19**	B	**39**	B		
20	C	**40**	C			**20**	B	**40**	C		

How to score your test

Each GED area test is scored on a scale of 100 - 200 points. To pass the GED, you must earn at least 145 on each of the four subject tests, for a total of at least 580 points (out of a possible 800).

Each subject test should be passed individually. It means that you must get 145 on each section of the test. If you failed one subject test but did well enough on another to get a total score of 580, that's still not a passing score.

There are four possible scores that you can receive on the GED Test:

Not Passing: This indicates that your score is lower than 145 on any of the four tests. If you do not pass, you can reschedule up to two times a year to retake any or all subjects of the GED test.

Passing Score/High School Equivalency: This score indicates that your score is between 145-164. Remember that points on one subject of the test do not carry over to the other subjects.

College Ready: This indicates that your score is between 165-175, demonstrating career and college readiness. A College Ready score shows that you may not need placement testing or remediation before beginning a college degree program.

College Ready + Credit: This indicates that your score is 175 or higher. This shows that you've already mastered some skills that would be taught in college courses. Depending on a school's policy, this can translate to some college credits—saving you time and money during your college education.

There are approximately 46 questions on GED Mathematical Reasoning. Similar to other subject areas, you will need a minimum score of 145 to pass the Mathematical Reasoning Test. There are 49 raw score points on the GED math test. The raw points correspond with correct answers. Most questions have one answer; therefore, they only have one point. There is more than one point for questions that have more than one answer. You'll get a raw score out of the 49 possible points. This will then be converted into your scaled score out of 200. Approximately, you need to get 32 out of 49 raw score to pass the Mathematical Reasoning section.

To score your GED Mathematical Reasoning practice tests, first find your raw score.

There were 46 questions on each GED Mathematical Reasoning practice test. All questions have one point except following questions that have 2 points:

GED Mathematical Reasoning practice test 1:

Question 30: Two points

Question 43: Two points

Question 44: Two points

GED Mathematical Reasoning practice test 2:

Question 18: Two points

Question 21: Two points

Question 27: Two points

Use the following table to convert GED Mathematical Reasoning raw score to scaled score.

GED Mathematical Reasoning raw score to scaled score	
Raw Scores	Scaled Scores
Below 32 (*not passing*)	*Below* 145
32 − 36	145 − 164
37 − 40	165 − 175
Above 40	*Above* 175

GED Mathematical Reasoning Practice Tests Answers and Explanations

Mathematical Reasoning Practice Test 1

Answers and Explanations

1) Choice D is correct

$3x - 5 = 8.5 \rightarrow 3x = 8.5 + 5 = 13.5 \rightarrow x = \frac{13.5}{3} = 4.5$

Then; $6x + 3 = 6\,(4.5) + 3 = 27 + 3 = 30$

2) Choice D is correct

First draw an isosceles triangle. Remember that two sides of the triangle are equal.

Let put a for the legs. Then:

$a = 8 \Rightarrow$ area of the triangle is $= \frac{1}{2}(8 \times 8) = \frac{64}{2} = 32 \; cm^2$

Isosceles right triangle

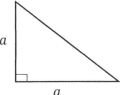

3) Choice D is correct

To find the discount, multiply the number by $(100\% - rate\ of\ discount)$.

Therefore, for the first discount we get: $(600)\,(100\% - 25\%) = (600)\,(0.75)$

For the next 15% discount: $(600)(0.75)(0.85)$

4) Choice A is correct

Plug in each pair of numbers in the equation: $3x + 5y = 11$

    A. $(2, 1)$: $3\,(2) + 5\,(1) = 11$
    B. $(-1, 2)$: $3\,(-1) + 5\,(2) = 7$
    C. $(-2, 2)$: $3\,(-2) + 5\,(2) = 4$
    D. $(2, 2)$: $3\,(2) + 5\,(2) = 16$

Choice A is correct.

5) The answer is -3.

Use PEMDAS (order of operation): $-15 + 6 \times (-5) - [4 + 22 \times (-4)] \div 2 =$

$-15 - 30 - [4 - 88] \div 2 = -45 - [-84] \div 2 = -45 + 84 \div 2 = -45 + 42 = -3$

6) Choice A is correct

Let x be the smallest number. Then, these are the numbers: $x, x + 1, x + 2, x + 3, x + 4$

average $= \frac{\text{sum of terms}}{\text{number of terms}} \Rightarrow 40 = \frac{x+(x+1)+(x+2)+(x+3)+(x+4)}{5} \Rightarrow 40 = \frac{5x+10}{5} \Rightarrow 200 = 5x + 10$
$\Rightarrow 190 = 5x \Rightarrow x = 38$

7) Choice C is correct

The area of the floor is: $7\ cm \times 24\ cm = 168\ cm^2$, The number of tiles needed $=$

$$168 \div 8 = 21$$

8) Choice C is correct

The weight of 15.2 meters of this rope is: $15.2 \times 600\ g = 9,120\ g$, $1\ kg = 1,000\ g$, therefore, $7,320\ g \div 1000 = 9.12\ kg$

9) Choice B is correct

6% of the volume of the solution is alcohol. Let x be the volume of the solution.

Then: $6\%\ of\ x = 24\ ml \Rightarrow 0.06\ x = 24 \Rightarrow x = 24 \div 0.06 = 400$

10) Choice B is correct

average $= \dfrac{\text{sum of terms}}{\text{number of terms}}$

The sum of the weight of all girls is: $18 \times 60 = 1080\ kg$, The sum of the weight of all boys is: $32 \times 62 = 1984\ kg$, The sum of the weight of all students is: $1080 + 1984 = 3064\ kg$

average $= \dfrac{3064}{50} = 61.28$

11) Choice C is correct

Let x be the original price. If the price of a laptop is decreased by 10% to $360, then:

$90\%\ of\ x = 360 \Rightarrow 0.90x = 360 \Rightarrow x = 360 \div 0.90 = 400$

12) Choice B is correct

Write the numbers in order: $4, 5, 8, 9, 13, 15, 18$

Since we have 7 numbers (7 is odd), then the median is the number in the middle, which is 9.

13) The answer is $1, 205. 76$

Surface Area of a cylinder $= 2\pi r\ (r + h)$,

The radius of the cylinder is 8 inches and its height is 12 inches. π is 3.14. Then:

Surface Area of a cylinder $= 2\ (3.14)\ (8)\ (8 + 16) = 1205.76$

14) Choice A is correct

Let x be the number of years. Therefore, $2,000$ *per year* equals $2000x$. starting from $27,000 annual salary means you should add that amount to $2000x$.

Income more than that is: $I > 2000x + 27000$

15) The answer is 5.

Solving Systems of Equations by Elimination

$3x - 4y = -20$
$-x + 2y = 10$ Multiply the second equation by 3, then add it to the first equation.

$\begin{array}{l} 3x - 4y = -20 \\ 3(-x + 2y = 10) \end{array} \Rightarrow \begin{array}{l} 3x - 4y = -20 \\ -3x + 6y = 30 \end{array} \Rightarrow 2y = 10 \Rightarrow y = 5$

16) Choice B is correct

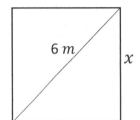

The diagonal of the square is 6 meters. Let x be the side.
Use Pythagorean Theorem: $a^2 + b^2 = c^2$
$x^2 + x^2 = 6^2 \Rightarrow 2x^2 = 6^2 \Rightarrow 2x^2 = 36 \Rightarrow x^2 = 18 \Rightarrow x = \sqrt{18}$
The area of the square is: $\sqrt{18} \times \sqrt{18} = 18 \, m^2$

17) Choice D is correct

If the length of the box is 24, then the width of the box is one third of it, 8, and the height of the box is 4 (half of the width). The volume of the box is: $V = lwh = (24)(8)(4) = 768$

18) Choice D is correct

Write the equation and solve for B: $0.60A = 0.20B$, divide both sides by 0.20, then:

$\frac{0.60}{0.20}A = B$, therefore: $B = 3A$, and B is 3 times of A or it's 300% of A.

19) The answer is 108.

To find the number of possible outfit combinations, multiply number of options for each factor:

$6 \times 3 \times 6 = 108$

20) Choice C is correct

Use simple interest formula: $I = prt$ ($I = interest,\ p = principal,\ r = rate,\ t = time$)

$I = (8,000)(0.025)(5) = 1,000$

21) The answer is 7,776

$6^5 = 6 \times 6 \times 6 \times 6 \times 6 = 7,776$

22) Choice B is correct

Use percent formula: $part = \frac{percent}{100} \times whole$. $15 = \frac{percent}{100} \times 20 \Rightarrow 15 = \frac{percent \times 20}{100} \Rightarrow$ $15 = \frac{percent \times 2}{10}$, multiply both sides by 10. $150 = percent \times 2$, divide both sides by 2. $75 = percent$

23) The answer is 78.

The perimeter of the trapezoid is 50. Therefore, the missing side (height) is $= 50 - 18 - 12 - 14 = 6$, Area of a trapezoid: $A = \frac{1}{2} h (b_1 + b_2) = \frac{1}{2} (6)(12 + 14) = 78$

24) Choice B is correct

Add the first 5 numbers. $40 + 45 + 50 + 35 + 55 = 225$

To find the distance traveled in the next 5 hours, multiply the average by number of hours.

Distance = Average × Rate $= 45 \times 5 = 225$,   Add both numbers. $225 + 225 = 450$

25) Choice B is correct

Use distance formula: $Distance = Rate \times time \Rightarrow 420 = 60 \times T$, divide both sides by 60. $\frac{420}{60} = T \Rightarrow T = 7 \ hours$

26) Choice D is correct.

Plug in each pair of numbers in the equation. The answer should be 20.

A. $(2, 1)$: $4(2) + 6(1) = 14$ No!
B. $(-1, 3)$: $4(-1) + 6(2) = 8$ No!
C. $(-2, 2)$: $4(-2) + 6(2) = 4$ No!
D. $(2, 2)$: $4(2) + 6(2) = 20$ Yes!

27) Choice C is correct

Let x be the number. Write the equation and solve for x.

$\frac{2}{3} \times 15 = \frac{2}{5} . x \Rightarrow \frac{2 \times 15}{3} = \frac{2x}{5}$, use cross multiplication to solve for x. $5 \times 30 = 2x \times 3 \Rightarrow$ $150 = 6x \Rightarrow x = 25$

28) Choice C is correct

To find the discount, multiply the number by $(100\% - rate\ of\ discount)$.

Therefore, for the first discount we get: $(D)(100\% - 20\%) = (D)(0.80) = 0.80\ D$

For increase of 15%: $(0.80D)(100\% + 15\%) = (0.80\ D)(1.15) = 0.92\ D = 92\%\ of\ D$

29) Choice B is correct

Use the formula for Percent of Change: $\frac{\text{New Value}-\text{Old Value}}{Old\ Value} \times 100\%$

$\frac{28-45}{45} \times 100\% = -37.7\%$ (negative sign here means that the new price is less than old price).

30) Choices D and E are correct

(If you selected 3 choices and 2 of them are correct, then you get one point. If you answered 2 or 3 choices and one of them is correct, you receive one point. If you selected more than 3 choices, you won't get any point for this question.)

Some of prime numbers are: $2, 3, 5, 7, 11, 13$. Find the product of two consecutive prime numbers: $2 \times 3 = 6$ (not in the options), $3 \times 5 = 15$ (bingo!), $5 \times 7 = 35$ (yes!) ,$7 \times 11 = 77$ (not in the options). Choices D and E are correct.

31) The answer is 160.

Th ratio of boy to girls is $2:3$. Therefore, there are 2 boys out of 5 students. To find the answer, first divide the total number of students by 5, then multiply the result by 2.

$400 \div 5 = 80 \Rightarrow 80 \times 2 = 160$

32) Choice B is correct

The question is this: 530.40 is what percent of 631? Use percent formula:

$\text{part} = \frac{\text{percent}}{100} \times \text{whole}$, $530.40 = \frac{\text{percent}}{100} \times 6331 \Rightarrow 530.40 = \frac{\text{percent} \times 631}{100} \Rightarrow$

$530.40 = percent \times 631 \Rightarrow percent = \frac{530.40}{631} = 84.05 \cong 84$

530.40 is 84% of 631. Therefore, the discount is: $100\% - 84\% = 16\%$

33) Choice B is correct

If the score of Mia was 60, therefore the score of Ava is 30. Since, the score of Emma was half as that of Ava, therefore, the score of Emma is 15.

34) Choice D is correct

If 20 balls are removed from the bag at random, there will be one ball in the bag. The probability of choosing a white ball is 1 out of 21. Therefore, the probability of not choosing a white ball is 20 out of 21 and the probability of having not a white ball after removing 20 balls is the same.

35) Choice D is correct

$8 \times 10 = 80$,   Petrol use: $10 \times 2 = 20$ liters,   Petrol cost: $20 \times 1 = 20$

Money earned: $80 - 20 = 60$

36) The answer is 52.

$$\text{average} = \frac{\text{sum of terms}}{\text{number of terms}} \Rightarrow 25 = \frac{13+15+20+x}{4} \Rightarrow 100 = 48 + x \Rightarrow x = 52$$

37) Choice C is correct

Let x be the original price. If the price of the sofa is decreased by 15% to \$476, then: 85% $of\ x = 476 \Rightarrow 0.85x = 476 \Rightarrow x = 476 \div 0.85 = 560$

38) Choice C is correct

Let x be the number. Write the equation and solve for x. $(28 - x) \div x = 3$

Multiply both sides by x. $(28 - x) = 3x$, then add x both sides. $28 = 4x$, now divide both sides by 4. $x = 7$

39) Choice C is correct

The sum of supplement angles is 180. Let x be that angle. Therefore, $x + 4x = 180$

$5x = 180$, divide both sides by 5: $x = 36$

40) Choice C is correct

The average speed of john is: $150 \div 6 = 25\ km$. The average speed of Alice is:

$160 \div 4 = 40\ km$. Write the ratio and simplify. $25:40 \Rightarrow 5:8$

41) Choice C is correct

Use Pythagorean Theorem: $a^2 + b^2 = c^2$

$5^2 + 12^2 = c^2 \Rightarrow 25 + 144 = c^2 \Rightarrow 169 = c^2 \Rightarrow c = 13$

42) Choice A is correct

The percent of girls take drawing class is: $75\% \times \frac{1}{3} = 25\%$

43) Choices A and B are correct

(If you selected 3 choices and 2 of them are correct, then you get one point. If you answered 2 or 3 choices and one of them is correct, you receive one point. If you selected more than 3 choices, you won't get any point for this question.)

Area of the circle is less than $14\ \pi$. Use the formula of areas of circles.

$Area = \pi r^2 \Rightarrow 49\ \pi > \pi r^2 \Rightarrow 49 > r^2 \Rightarrow r < 7$

Radius of the circle is less than 7. Let's put 7 for the radius. Now, use the circumference formula: $Circumference\ = 2\pi r = 2\pi\ (7) = 14\pi$. Since the radius of the circle is less than 7. Then, the circumference of the circle must be less than 14π. Only choices A and B are less than 14π.

44) Choice D and E are correct

Simplify the inequality: $2y + 6 < 30 \rightarrow 2y < 30 - 6 \rightarrow 2y < 24 \rightarrow y < 12$. Only choices D (8) and E (-12) are less than 12.

45) Choice C is correct

The question is this: 185.00 is what percent of 125.00? Use percent formula:

$\frac{185}{125} = 1.48$ or 148%

46) Choice B is correct

Use the information provided in the question to draw the shape.

Use Pythagorean Theorem: $a^2 + b^2 = c^2$

$80^2 + 150^2 = c^2 \Rightarrow 6{,}400 + 22{,}500 = c^2 \Rightarrow 28{,}900 = c^2 \Rightarrow c = 170$

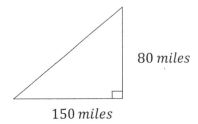

$80\ miles$

$150\ miles$

GED Mathematical Reasoning Practice Test 2

Answers and Explanations

1) The answer is: -64

Use PEMDAS (order of operation): $[3 \times (-14) - 48] - 14 + [3 \times 8] \div 2 =$

$$[-42 - 48] + 14 + 24 \div 2 = -90 + 14 + 12 = -64$$

2) Choice A is correct

Write a proportion and solve for the missing number. $\frac{32}{12} = \frac{6}{x} \rightarrow 32x = 6 \times 12 = 72$

$32x = 72 \rightarrow x = \dfrac{72}{32} = 2.25$

3) Choice A is correct

To solve absolute values equations, write two equations. $2x - 6$ can equal positive 12, or negative 12. Therefore, $2x - 6 = 12 \Rightarrow 2x = 18 \Rightarrow x = 9$.

$2x - 6 = -12 \Rightarrow 2x = -12 + 6 = -6 \Rightarrow x = -3$.

Find the product of solutions: $-3 \times 9 = -27$

4) Choice B is correct

The equation of a line in slope intercept form is: $y = mx + b$. Solve for y. $3x - y = 6 \rightarrow$

$-y = -3x + 6$. Divide both sides by (-1). Then: $-y = -3x + 6 \rightarrow y = 3x - 6$

The slope of this line is 3. The product of the slopes of two perpendicular lines is -1. Therefore, the slope of a line that is perpendicular to this line is:

$$m_1 \times m_2 = -1 \Rightarrow 3 \times m_2 = -1 \Rightarrow m_2 = \frac{-1}{3} = -\frac{1}{3}$$

5) Choice C is correct

Plug in the value of x and y. $3(x - 2y) + (2 - x)^2$ when $x = 5$ and $y = -3$

$3(x - 2y) + (2 - x)^2 = 3(5 - 2(-3)) + (2 - 5)^2 = 3(5 + 6) + (-3)^2 = 33 + 9 = 42$

6) The answer is 2.5

First, use distribute property to simplify $-4(x + 2)$. $-4(x + 2) = -4x - 8$

Now, combine like terms: $x - 4(x + 2) = -15.5 \rightarrow x - 4x - 8 = -15.5 \rightarrow -3x - 8 = -15.5$

Add 8 to both sides of the equation: $-3x - 8 + 8 = -15.5 + 8 \rightarrow -3x = -7.5$. Divide both sides by -3. Then: $-3x = -7.5 \rightarrow \frac{-3x}{-3} = \frac{-7.5}{-3} \rightarrow x = 2.5$

7) Choice D is correct

Solve for x. $x - 4 \leq 4x - 8 < 16 \Rightarrow$ (add 8 all sides) $-4 + 8 < 4x - 8 + 8 < 16 + 8 \Rightarrow$

$4 < 4x < 24 \Rightarrow$ (divide all sides by 4) $1 \leq x < 6$

x is between 1 and 6. Choice D represents this inequality.

8) Choice D is correct

$Volume\ of\ a\ box\ =\ length \times width \times height = 4 \times 5 \times 6 = 120$

9) Choice A is correct

Simplify and combine like terms. $(6x^3 - 8x^2 + 2x^4) - (4x^2 - 2x^4 + 2x^3) \Rightarrow$
$(6x^3 - 8x^2 + 2x^4) - 4x^2 + 2x^4 - 2x^3 \Rightarrow 4x^4 + 4x^3 - 12x^2$

10) Choice C is correct

the population is increased by 15% and 20%. 15% increase changes the population to 115% of original population. For the second increase, multiply the result by 120%.

$(1.15) \times (1.20) = 1.38 = 138\%$. 38 percent of the population is increased after two years.

11) Choice C is correct

Three times of 24,000 is 72,000. One sixth of them cancelled their tickets.

One sixth of 72,000 equals 12,000 ($\frac{1}{6} \times 72,000 = 12,000$).

60,000 ($72000 - 12,000 = 60,000$) fans are attending this week

12) The answer is 97.6

The area of the square is 595.36. Therefore, the side of the square is square root of the area.

$\sqrt{595.36} = 24.4$.   Four times the side of the square is the perimeter: $4 \times 24.4 = 97.6$

13) Choice D is correct

Change the numbers to decimal and then compare. $\frac{2}{3} = 0.666..., 0.68, 67\% = 0.67, \frac{4}{5} = 0.80$

Therefore: $\frac{2}{3} < 67\% < 0.68 < \frac{4}{5}$

14) Choice C is correct

average (mean) $= \frac{\text{sum of terms}}{\text{number of terms}} \Rightarrow 88 = \frac{\text{sum of terms}}{50} \Rightarrow sum = 88 \times 50 = 4,400$

The difference of 94 and 69 is 25. Therefore, 25 should be subtracted from the sum.

$4400 - 25 = 4,375$, mean $\frac{\text{sum of terms}}{\text{number of terms}} \Rightarrow mean = \frac{4,375}{50} = 87.5$

15) Choice B is correct

For sum of 5: (1 & 4) *and* (4 & 1), (2 & 3) and (3 & 2), therefore we have 4 options.
For sum of 8: (5 & 3) *and* (3 & 5), (4 & 4) and (2 & 6), *and* (6 & 2). There are 5 options. To get a sum of 5 or 8 for two dice: $4 + 5 = 9$
Since, we have $6 \times 6 = 36$ total number of options, the probability of getting a sum of 5 and 8 is 11 out of 36 or $\frac{11}{36} = \frac{1}{4}$

16) The answer is 8.

Use formula of rectangle prism volume. $V = (length)(width)(height) \Rightarrow$

$2000 = (25)(10)(height) \Rightarrow height = 2,000 \div 250 = 8$

17) Choice C is correct

To find the number of possible outfit combinations, multiply number of options for each factor:

$3 \times 5 \times 4 = 60$

18) Choices A and B are correct

(If you selected 3 choices and 2 of them are correct, then you get one point. If you answered 2 or 3 choices and one of them is correct, you receive one point. If you selected more than 3 choices, you won't get any point for this question.)

In the stadium the ratio of home fans to visiting fans in a crowd is $5:7$. Therefore, total number of fans must be divisible by $12: 5 + 7 = 12$.

Let's review the choices:

◻A. 12,324: $12,324 \div 12 = 1,027$

◻B. 16,788: $16,788 \div 12 = 1,399$

◻C. 42,326 $42,326 \div 12 = 3,527.166$

◻D. 44,566 $44,566 \div 12 = 3,713.833$

◻E. 66,812 $66,812 \div 12 = 5,567.66666$

Only choices A and B when divided by 12 result a whole number.

19) Choice B is correct

The diagonal of the square is 8. Let x be the side.

Use Pythagorean Theorem: $a^2 + b^2 = c^2$

$x^2 + x^2 = 8^2 \Rightarrow 2x^2 = 8^2 \Rightarrow 2x^2 = 64 \Rightarrow x^2 = 32 \Rightarrow x = \sqrt{32}$

The area of the square is: $\sqrt{32} \times \sqrt{32} = 32$

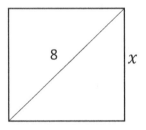

20) Choice B is correct

$$\text{Probability} = \frac{number\ of\ desired\ outcomes}{number\ of\ total\ outcomes} = \frac{18}{12+18+18+24} = \frac{18}{72} = \frac{1}{4}$$

21) Choices A and E are correct

(If you selected 3 choices and 2 of them are correct, then you get one point. If you answered 2 or 3 choices and one of them is correct, you receive one point. If you selected more than 3 choices, you won't get any point for this question.)

$x + 2y = 4$. Plug in the values of x and y from choices provided. Then:

◻A. $(-2, 3)$ $x + 2y = 4 \rightarrow -2 + 2(3) = 4 \rightarrow -2 + 6 = 4$ This is true!

◻B. $(1, 2)$ $x + 2y = 4 \rightarrow 1 + 2(2) = 4 \rightarrow 1 + 4 = 5$ This is NOT true!

◻C. $(-1, 3)$ $x + 2y = 4 \rightarrow -1 + 2(3) = 4 \rightarrow -1 + 6 = 5$ This is NOT true!

◻D. $(-3, 4)$ $x + 2y = 4 \rightarrow -3 + 2(4) = 4 \rightarrow -3 + 8 = 5$ This is NOT true!

◻E. $(0, 2)$ $x + 2y = 4 \rightarrow 0 + 2(2) = 4 \rightarrow 4 = 4$ This is true!

22) Choice A is correct

The width of the rectangle is twice its length. Let x be the length. Then, $width = 2x$

Perimeter of the rectangle is $2 \, (width + length) \; = 2(2x + x) = 60 \Rightarrow 6x = 60 \; \Rightarrow \; x = 10$

Length of the rectangle is 10 meters.

23) Choice D is correct

average $= \dfrac{\text{sum of terms}}{\text{number of terms}} \Rightarrow$ (average of 6 numbers) $12 = \dfrac{\text{sum of numbers}}{6} \Rightarrow$ sum of 6 numbers is $12 \times 6 = 72$

(average of 4 numbers) $\; 10 = \dfrac{\text{sum of numbers}}{4} \Rightarrow$ sum of 4 numbers is $10 \times 4 \; = 40$

$sum \; of \; 6 \; numbers - \; sum \; of \; 4 \; numbers \; = \; sum \; of \; 2 \; numbers, \; 72 - 40 \; = 32,$

average of 2 numbers $= \dfrac{32}{2} = 16$

24) Choice C is correct

Solving Systems of Equations by Elimination

Multiply the first equation by (-2), then add it to the second equation.

$\begin{array}{l} -2(2x + 5y = \; 11) \\ \underline{\;\;\; 4x - 2y = -14 \;\;\;} \end{array} \Rightarrow \begin{array}{l} -4x - 10y = \; -22 \\ \underline{\;\;\; 4x - 2y = -14} \end{array} \Rightarrow -12y = \; -36 \Rightarrow y = \; 3$

Plug in the value of y into one of the equations and solve for x.

$2x + 5(3) = 11 \Rightarrow 2x + 15 = 11 \Rightarrow 2x = -4 \Rightarrow x = -2$

25) Choice B is correct

The perimeter of the trapezoid is $36 \; cm$.

Therefore, the missing side (height) is $= 36 - 8 - 12 - 6 \; = 10$

Area of a trapezoid: $A \; = \frac{1}{2} \, h \, (b_1 + \; b_2) = \frac{1}{2} \, (10) \, (6 \; + \; 8) \; = 70$

26) Choice B is correct

The probability of choosing a Hearts is $\dfrac{13}{52} = \dfrac{1}{4}$

27) Choices D and E are correct

(If you selected 3 choices and 2 of them are correct, then you get one point. If you answered 2 or 3 choices and one of them is correct, you receive one point. If you selected more than 3 choices, you won't get any point for this question.)

First, find the sum of five numbers.

$$\text{average} \ = \frac{\text{sum of terms}}{\text{number of terms}} \Rightarrow 25 = \frac{\text{sum of 5 numbers}}{5} \Rightarrow \text{sum of 5 numbers} = 25 \times 5 \ = 125$$

The sum of 5 numbers is 125. If a sixth number that is greater than 42 is added to these numbers, then the sum of 6 numbers must be greater than 162. $125 + 42 = 167$

If the number was 42, then the average of the numbers is:

$$\text{average} \ = \frac{\text{sum of terms}}{\text{number of terms}} = \frac{167}{6} = 27.83$$

Since the number is bigger than 42. Then, the average of six numbers must be greater than 27.83.

Choices D and E are greater than 27.83.

28) The answer is 28.

Let x be the width of the rectangle. Use Pythagorean Theorem:

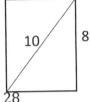

$$a^2 + b^2 = c^2$$

$$x^2 + 8^2 = 10^2 \Rightarrow x^2 + 64 \ = 100 \Rightarrow x^2 = 100 - 64 \ = 36 \Rightarrow x \ = 6$$

Perimeter of the rectangle $= \ 2\ (length \ + \ width) \ = 2\ (8 \ + \ 6) = 2\ (14) = 28$

29) Choice C is correct

Th ratio of boy to girls is $4:7$. Therefore, there are 4 boys out of 11 students. To find the answer, first divide the total number of students by 11, then multiply the result by 4. $44 \div 11 = 4 \Rightarrow 4 \times 4 \ = 16$. There are 16 boys and $28\ (44-16)$ girls. So, 12 more boys should be enrolled to make the ratio $1:1$

30) Choice A is correct

2,500 out of 55,000 equals to $\dfrac{2500}{55000} = \dfrac{25}{550} = \dfrac{1}{22}$

31) The answer is 60.

Jason needs an 75% average to pass for five exams. Therefore, the sum of 5 exams must be at lease $5 \times 75 = 375$. The sum of 4 exams is: $68 + 72 + 85 \ + \ 90 \ = 315$.

The minimum score Jason can earn on his fifth and final test to pass is: $375 - 315 = 60$

32) Choice D is correct

Isolate and solve for x. $\dfrac{2}{3}x + \dfrac{1}{6} = \dfrac{1}{3} \Rightarrow \dfrac{2}{3}x \ = \ \dfrac{1}{3} - \dfrac{1}{6} = \dfrac{1}{6} \Rightarrow \dfrac{2}{3}x = \dfrac{1}{6}$

Multiply both sides by the reciprocal of the coefficient of x. $\left(\dfrac{3}{2}\right)\dfrac{2}{3}x = \dfrac{1}{6}\left(\dfrac{3}{2}\right) \Rightarrow x \ = \ \dfrac{3}{12} = \dfrac{1}{4}$

33) Choice B is correct

Use simple interest formula: $I = prt$ (I = interest, p = principal, r = rate, t = time)

$I = (12000)(0.035)(2) = 840$

34) Choice D is correct

Simplify. $6x^2y^3(2x^2y)^3 = 6x^2y^3(8x^6y^3) = 48x^8y^6$

35) Choice C is correct

Surface Area of a cylinder $= 2\pi r \ (r \ + \ h)$, The radius of the cylinder is 3 $(6 \div 2)$ inches and its height is 8 inches. Therefore, Surface Area of a cylinder $= 2\pi \ (3) \ (3 \ + \ 8) \ = 66 \ \pi$

36) Choice C is correct

The square of a number is $\frac{25}{64}$, then the number is the square root of $\frac{25}{64}$. $\sqrt{\frac{25}{64}} = \frac{5}{8}$

The cube of the number is: $(\frac{5}{8})^3 = \frac{125}{512}$

37) Choice B is correct

Write the numbers in order: $2, 19, 27, 28, 35, 44, 67$.

Median is the number in the middle. So, the median is 28.

38) The answer is 170.

Use the information provided in the question to draw the shape.

Use Pythagorean Theorem: $a^2 + b^2 = c^2$

$80^2 + 150^2 = c^2 \Rightarrow 6400 + 22500 = c^2 \Rightarrow 28900 = c^2 \Rightarrow c = 170$

150 miles

Port A

80 miles

39) Choice B is correct

Plug in 104 for F and then solve for C. $C \ = \ \frac{5}{9} \ (F - 32) \Rightarrow C \ = \ \frac{5}{9} \ (104 - 32) \Rightarrow$

$C = \frac{5}{9} \ (72) \ = \ 40$

40) Choice C is correct

Let x be the number. Write the equation and solve for x. $40\% \ of \ x = 4 \Rightarrow 0.40 \ x = 4 \Rightarrow x = 4 \div 0.40 = 10$

41) Choice D is correct

Let x be all expenses, then $\frac{22}{100}x = \$660 \rightarrow x = \frac{100 \times \$660}{22} = \$3,000$. He spent for his rent: $\frac{27}{100} \times \$3,000 = \$810$

42) Choice C is correct

The distance between Jason and Joe is 9 miles. Jason running at 5.5 miles per hour and Joe is running at the speed of 7 miles per hour. Therefore, every hour the distance is 1.5 miles less.

$9 \div 1.5 = 6$

43) Choice D is correct

The failing rate is 11 out of 55 = $\frac{11}{55}$. Change the fraction to percent: $\frac{11}{55} \times 100\% = 20\%$

20 percent of students failed. Therefore, 80 percent of students passed the exam.

44) Choice A is correct

First, find the number. Let x be the number. Write the equation and solve for x.

150% of a number is 75, then: $1.5 \times x = 75 \Rightarrow x = 75 \div 1.5 = 50$

90% of 50 is: $0.9 \times 50 = 45$

45) The answer is 2.

Solve for y. $4x - 2y = 6 \Rightarrow -2y = 6 - 4x \Rightarrow y = 2x - 3$. The slope of the line is 2.

46) Choice A is correct

Let x be the number of new shoes the team can purchase. Therefore, the team can purchase $120\,x$. The team had $20,000 and spent $14,000. Now the team can spend on new shoes $6,000 at most. Now, write the inequality: $120x + 14,000 \leq 20,000$

"Effortless Math Education" Publications

Effortless Math authors' team strives to prepare and publish the best quality GED Mathematics learning resources to make learning Math easier for all. We hope that our publications help you learn Math in an effective way and prepare for the GED test.

We all in Effortless Math wish you good luck and successful studies!

Effortless Math Authors

Visit www.EffortlessMath.com
for Online Math Practice

www.EffortlessMath.com

… So Much More Online!

✓ FREE Math lessons

✓ More Math learning books!

✓ Mathematics Worksheets

✓ Online Math Tutors

Need a PDF version of this book?

Visit www.EffortlessMath.com

Made in the USA
Monee, IL
27 October 2020